Chihuahuan Desert National Parks Reptile and Amphibian Inventory

Natural Resource Technical Report NPS/CHDN/NRTR—2011/489

Authors:

Dave Prival and Matt Goode
School of Natural Resources
University of Arizona

Editors:

Ann Lewis
Physical Science Laboratory
New Mexico State University

M. Hildegard Reiser
Chihuahuan Desert Inventory & Monitoring Program
National Park Service

September 2011

U.S. Department of the Interior
National Park Service
Natural Resource Stewardship and Science
Fort Collins, Colorado

The National Park Service, Natural Resource Stewardship and Science office in Fort Collins, Colorado publishes a range of reports that address natural resource topics of interest and applicability to a broad audience in the National Park Service and others in natural resource management, including scientists, conservation and environmental constituencies, and the public.

The Natural Resource Technical Report Series is used to disseminate results of scientific studies in the physical, biological, and social sciences for both the advancement of science and the achievement of the National Park Service mission. The series provides contributors with a forum for displaying comprehensive data that are often deleted from journals because of page limitations.

All manuscripts in the series receive the appropriate level of peer review to ensure that the information is scientifically credible, technically accurate, appropriately written for the intended audience, and designed and published in a professional manner.

This report received informal peer review by subject-matter experts who were not directly involved in the collection, analysis, or reporting of the data. Data in this report were collected and analyzed using methods based on established, peer-reviewed protocols and were analyzed and interpreted within the guidelines of the protocols.

Views, statements, findings, conclusions, recommendations, and data in this report do not necessarily reflect views and policies of the National Park Service, U.S. Department of the Interior. Mention of trade names or commercial products does not constitute endorsement or recommendation for use by the U.S. Government.

This report is available from the Chihuahuan Desert Network website (http://science.nature.nps.gov/im/units/chdn/index.cfm) and the Natural Resource Publications Management website (http://www.nature.nps.gov/publications/nrpm/).

Please cite this publication as:

Prival, D., and M. Goode. 2011. Chihuahuan Desert National Parks reptile and amphibian inventory. Natural Resource Technical Report NPS/CHDN/NRTR—2011/489. National Park Service, Fort Collins, Colorado.

NPS 960/110293, September 2011

Contents

Contents (continued)

Contents (continued)

Figures

Figures (continued)

Tables

Acknowledgments

We would like to specially acknowledge those who did the sweating and bleeding on this inventory — James Borgmeyer, Brett DeGregorio, Adrienne Dreyfus, Allison Ebner, Dave Furphy, Whitny Howeth, Dan Moen, Ian Murray, Chris Newsom, Barry Stephenson, Damon and Eliot Stone, Mike Swink, Chris Teske, and Mike Woolman. We thank our park contacts for doing all they could to make this project a success – Rick Slade and Joe LaBadie at AMIS, Raymond Skiles and Melissa Powell at BIBE, Dave Roemer at CAVE, John Heiner at FODA, Fred Armstrong and John Richter at GUMO, and Bill Conrod at WHSA.

We would also like to thank Melissa Amarello, Val Catt, Carol Debis-Harrell, Alejandro Diaz, Suzie Ehret, Lee Fitzgerald, Tom Giermakowski, Dave Hays, Donna Laing, Jim Mueller, Larry Norris, Lyz Oakley, Bill Reid, Hildy Reiser, Dee Simmons, and Cecily Westphal for their assistance and support.

We also wish to express our sincere apprectiation to Jack Skiles for allowing us access to part of AMIS through his private land.

We thank the National Park Service for funding this inventory, and the University of Arizona School of Natural Resources for providing administrative support.

Introduction

The primary mission of the National Park Service (NPS) is to manage national parks to "…conserve the scenery and natural and historic objects and the wild life therein and to provide for the enjoyment of the same in such manner and by such means as will leave them unimpaired for the enjoyment of future generations." (U.S. Congress: 39 Stat. 535). Although this mission has been in place for almost 90 years, few parks have conducted thorough inventories of their natural resources, and even fewer have attempted to conduct any kind of monitoring to determine whether management practices conflict with their primary mission (Stohlgren et al. 1995).

A reasonable first step toward conserving natural resources in parks, therefore, is to simply figure out what those natural resources are. In the late 1990s, the NPS began a program to take this first step and inventory the vascular plants and vertebrates (i.e., mammals, birds, reptiles, and amphibians) that inhabit each park with significant natural resources.

As part of this nationwide effort, the Chihuahuan Desert Network (Figure 1) of the NPS entered into a cooperative agreement with the School of Natural Resources at the University of Arizona to conduct a two-year inventory of reptiles and amphibians in six network parks – Amistad National Recreation Area, TX (AMIS), Big Bend National Park, TX (BIBE), Carlsbad Caverns National Park, NM (CAVE), Fort Davis National Historic Site, TX (FODA), Guadalupe Mountains National Park, TX (GUMO), and White Sands National Monument, NM (WHSA). This inventory took place from May to September 2003 and June to September 2004.

Although reptile and amphibian diversity within these parks was expected to be high, reliable species lists did not exist for most parks, and little information was available regarding the distribution of herpetofauna, including species of special conservation concern (Stohlgren and Quinn 1992). This baseline information is essential to guide decisions regarding the use of particular areas for interpretive, recreational, or other purposes, and to allow for the development of effective monitoring programs.

A stated goal of the NPS national inventory effort is to document 90% of all vertebrate and vascular plant species occurring in every park in the United States. Because most reptile and amphibian species are inconspicuous, secretive, well camouflaged, present in very low densities, and/or concealed and inactive for most of the year, documenting 90% of all species in any park is extremely difficult. In effect, our primary goal was simply to document as many reptile and amphibian species as possible within each park. To determine if we reached the 90% goal, we compared our findings with lists of species we believe are likely to occur in each park based upon previous sightings, museum records, and species range maps and habitat preferences. It is important to note that we have a very incomplete set of museum records at our disposal, so some guesswork was involved in determining what species are likely to occur in each park. In order to augment our inventory efforts, a complete analysis of existing museum data will be performed by NPS personnel in the future.

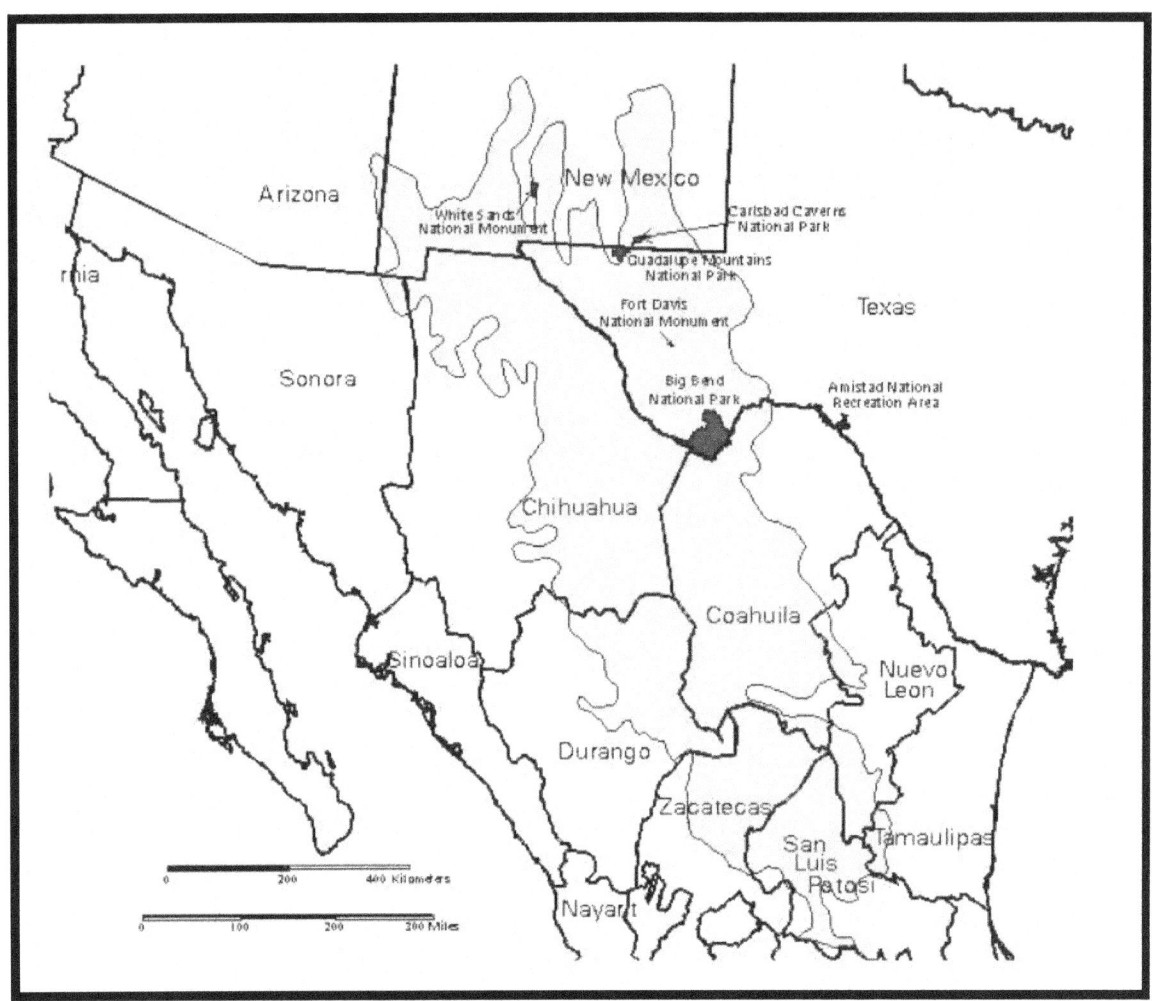

Figure 1. Locations of surveyed national parks within the Chihuahuan Desert ecoregion.

Our secondary objective was to map the distributions of all species we found within each park, because these data have great potential for use in future monitoring efforts. Finally, we set out to obtain rough relative abundance data for the herp species in all parks, which may also prove important for monitoring efforts.

This report documents the results of our inventory for both years. We describe the methods used for finding reptiles and amphibians and documenting their presence and distribution, the results of our surveys on a park-by-park basis, and present options for future monitoring efforts.

Methods

The bulk of our inventory effort consisted of foot searches. However, we also utilized road cruising, pitfall traps, turtle traps, and recorded data for every reptile and amphibian we saw incidentally. Generally we focused our search efforts on areas of high reptile and amphibian diversity, while also covering as many areas of each park as possible in order to document species distributions. At BIBE, however, due to the size of the park and the fact that many of the most diverse areas are already well known herpetologically, we focused our efforts primarily on three mountain ranges that had not been previously surveyed.

Foot Searches

Foot searches involved surveying pre-defined areas during periods when reptiles and amphibians were most likely to be active. Generally, we conducted foot searches between 0730 and 1200 to document diurnal snakes and lizards, and between 1800 and 2400 to document amphibians and nocturnal snakes and lizards. Actual start and end times varied depending upon time of sunrise/sunset, weather, and the elevation of the search area.

During a similar inventory of Sonoran Desert National Parks in 2001 (Prival et al. 2001), we initially used randomly placed plots to survey for reptiles and amphibians. In theory, this approach is desirable from a statistical perspective, because it allows for inferences to be drawn to the entire park from a randomly selected sample, therefore, being more useful in a monitoring context. However, we learned that this is a highly ineffective method for conducting inventories in parks (unless those parks are very small and homogenous), because reptiles and amphibians are not randomly distributed. As a result, using a randomized approach results in expending a great deal of time and effort to reach inaccessible places where, in most cases, diversity and abundance are low.

Therefore, during this study we focused our efforts on areas we believed were most likely to support high diversity or rare species. We concentrated largely on canyons and riparian areas, but attempted to make sure that all habitat types within each park were represented in searches. We varied our search areas as much as possible to increase our distribution data without compromising our primary goal of documenting as many species as possible.

Occasionally we searched trails during foot searches, but most of the time we searched off-trail. In addition to simply looking around as we walked, we looked under rocks and logs and used mirrors and flashlights to illuminate crevices. Whenever cover was moved, we replaced it exactly as found.

During each search, we recorded the name of the area, start and end times, and weather (air temperature at 1.5 meters [4.9 ft], relative humidity, and cloud cover) at the beginning and end of the search. We also recorded the boundaries of the search area in such a way that the same area could be searched again in the future.

Whenever we found a reptile or amphibian, we recorded the species, subspecies (if identifiable), time, habitat (dry canyon bottom, slope, ridgetop/peak, flats, riparian, cliff wall, sand dune, lake, or cave), substrate (ground, vegetation, rock, structure, burrow, water, under cover, or crevice), and age (adult/juvenile or neonate/hatchling). In 2004, we added "terrace" to the habitat category and "road" to the substrate category as options.

We also recorded the location of every reptile and amphibian found using a Global Positioning System (GPS) unit, using WGS 84 as our datum. Our crew recorded all of this information into Palm Pilots using a datasheet in Pendragon Forms, which could be downloaded into a laptop, reducing the likelihood of transcription errors. This method of collecting data also greatly reduced time spent on data entry, which enabled us to spend more time conducting surveys.

Unfortunately, recording our data directly onto computers did cause a problem at AMIS in 2004, where we lost 14 person-days of data when a park computer crashed. We were able to reconstruct the snake data from memory, but lost many lizard and amphibian observations. We also lost an unknown number of person-days at WHSA in 2004, possibly due to a long delay between recording data and downloading it onto a computer. Fortunately, no data regarding new species for either park were lost.

Incidental Observations

To supplement our other search methods, we obtained data for every reptile and amphibian we saw in a park while we were not conducting a formalized search. For example, we often observed animals when we were driving in a park to a search area, walking around the housing area, or enjoying a hike on a day off. These animals were recorded as "incidentals." We recorded the same information about each animal, including GPS coordinates, as described above in the "Foot Searches" section.

Road Cruising

Road cruising involves slowly driving along a road at night in order to find amphibians and nocturnal snakes and lizards. During road cruising surveys, we recorded the names of the roads driven, start and end times, number of miles driven, and weather (air temperature at 1.5 meters [4.9 ft], relative humidity, and cloud cover) at the beginning and end of the survey. Whenever we found a reptile or amphibian, we recorded the species, subspecies (if identifiable), time, whether the animal was dead or alive (or, in 2004, injured), and GPS coordinates. In general, we did not spend a great deal of time road cruising due to a lack of suitable roads in most parks and in order to obtain better distribution data.

Pitfall Traps

Pitfall traps are used to capture small reptiles and amphibians, and although they don't usually capture large numbers of animals, they can be especially useful for finding nocturnal, secretive animals and fossorial species. A pitfall trap array consists of four 5-gallon buckets, each completely sunken into the ground. The buckets are connected by low walls (each approximately 10 meters [32.8 ft] in length) constructed of silt fencing, such that three of the buckets connect to a central bucket in a triangular configuration. Placing the silt-fencing wall in the ground involves digging a shallow (ca. 15.2 cm [6 in]) trench and then using stakes to secure the wall in place. Animals running or crawling across the ground come to one of the walls and turn left or right. Whichever way they turn, they reach an open bucket into which they fall.

Our park contacts, other park personnel, and several volunteers generously assisted us in the labor-intensive process of installing pitfall arrays. In 2003, we installed two arrays at AMIS, three arrays at CAVE, two arrays at FODA, two arrays at GUMO (one with only two walls instead of the usual three), and three arrays at WHSA. In addition, Mike Swink and Bill Conrod installed two more one-wall arrays at WHSA, and Mike Swink added funnel traps to these two arrays. Also, Rick Slade and Whitny Howeth installed a third array at AMIS. In 2004, we installed two more arrays at GUMO.

As requested by park staff, the FODA, GUMO, and WHSA pitfall arrays were dismantled at the end of the project. The AMIS and CAVE arrays remain available for use in future monitoring efforts.

Because our crew was spread between six parks and we were often searching areas far from the pitfall arrays, park staff and volunteers typically checked the pitfalls for us. We did not install pitfall arrays at BIBE because nobody was available to check them on a regular basis.

Initially, the buckets were kept closed during the day and only opened at night in order to ensure that no animals became overheated in a bucket due to the sun. This meant that the arrays had to be visited twice a day – late in the afternoon to remove the bucket lids, and early in the morning to check the traps and close them. Later in the 2003 season, park personnel constructed boards with 2.5 to 5.1 cm long legs (1 to 2 in) that could be used to shade the buckets at most of the parks. Pitfall arrays with shade boards only had to be checked once a day because the lids could be left off at all times.

Turtle Traps

At AMIS, we occasionally used turtle traps to document the species of turtles living in the reservoir. We staked hoop traps into shallow water with PVC pipe and baited the traps with sardines in order to attract and capture turtles. These traps were checked daily when in use. In 2003, after temporarily using turtle traps during a canoe trip along the Devils River, we stationed three traps in the reservoir by Diablo East, where they were run by Whitny Howeth.

Due to the rapidly fluctuating water level in the reservoir, Whitny had to move the traps often. On July 3, the water level rose rapidly enough to result in the death by drowning of four turtles before the traps were checked the next morning. Clearly, the reservoir is a particularly challenging place in which to run turtle traps.

We did not attempt to trap turtles at BIBE, because park personnel suggested that we spend most of our time in remote areas of the park that had not been previously surveyed. In addition, a substantial amount of work has focused on turtles inhabiting the Rio Grande. At CAVE, we did not trap for turtles at Rattlesnake Springs, because we felt that we could adequately survey the pond visually by observing basking turtles and the steep sides of the pond are not conducive to the use of turtle traps.

Search Effort

In 2003, our crew, Mike Woolman (at CAVE), and Adrienne Dreyfus (at FODA) spent 62 person-days at AMIS, 79 at BIBE, 157 at CAVE, 51 at FODA, 79 at GUMO, and 27 at WHSA for a total of 455 person-days in the field. In 2004, our crew and Chris Newsom (at CAVE) spent 72 person-days at AMIS, 52 at BIBE, 54 at CAVE, 18 at FODA, 74 at GUMO, and 15 at WHSA, for a total of 285 person-days in the field.

The allotment of time spent at each park changed somewhat from our original proposal based on a variety of factors such as logistics, weather, and our increasing familiarity with parks and their needs.

Our foot search effort, and the effort of Mike Woolman and Chris Newsom at CAVE and Adrienne Dreyfus at FODA, is detailed in Table 1. The 2003 field season, lasting from May 5 to September 29, was significantly longer than the 2004 field season, which only lasted from June 14 to September 16.

In 2003, we conducted two road-cruising surveys at AMIS, 11 at BIBE, one at CAVE, six at GUMO, and one at WHSA. Mike Woolman conducted 50 road-cruising surveys at CAVE. In 2004, we conducted two road-cruising surveys at AMIS, 25 at BIBE, two at CAVE, 10 at GUMO, and one at WHSA. Chris Newsom conducted 20 road-cruising surveys at CAVE. No road-cruising surveys were conducted at FODA due to a lack of paved roads.

During 2003, the AMIS pitfall traps were checked 12 times, the CAVE traps 110 times, the FODA traps 26 times, the GUMO traps 35 times, and the WHSA traps 58 times. During 2004, the AMIS traps were checked 21 times, the CAVE traps 10 times, the FODA traps 10 times, the GUMO traps 90 times (arrays 1 and 2 only; arrays 3 and 4 were checked 11 times), and the WHSA traps 26 times (although not all traps were checked each time).

Turtle traps at AMIS were checked 27 times in 2003. In 2004, we ran turtle traps for 11 days.

Table 1. Foot search effort.

Park	Year	Number of Foot Searches	Number of Person-hours	Average Number of Hours per Search
AMIS	2003	107	311.8	2.9
AMIS*	2004	> 97	> 264.3	2.7
AMIS TOTAL *	**2003-04**	**> 204**	**> 576.1**	**2.8**
BIBE	2003	74	286.9	3.9
BIBE	2004	54	160.2	3.0
BIBE TOTAL	**2003-04**	**128**	**447.1**	**3.5**

Table1. Foot search effort (continued).

Park	Year	Number of Foot Searches	Number of Person-hours	Average Number of Hours per Search
CAVE (our crew)	2003	100	348.2	3.5
CAVE (Mike Woolman)	2003	105	273.2	2.6
CAVE (our crew)	2004	11	26.5	2.4
CAVE (Chris Newsom and Dave Roemer)	2004	55	85.6	1.6
CAVE TOTAL	**2003-04**	**271**	**733.5**	**2.7**
FODA (our crew)	2003	56	207.0	3.7
FODA (Adrienne Dreyfus)	2003	29	34.8	1.2
FODA	2004	20	56.9	2.8
FODA TOTAL	**2003-04**	**105**	**298.7**	**2.8**
GUMO	2003	100	462.7	4.6
GUMO	2004	108	361.8	3.4
GUMO TOTAL	**2003-04**	**208**	**824.5**	**4.0**
WHSA	2003	37	97.1	2.6
WHSA**	2004	>13	>40.2	3.1
WHSA TOTAL**	**2003-04**	**>50**	**>137.3**	**2.7**

* Because 14 person-days of data were lost, actual search effort was higher than indicated here.
** Because an unknown number of person-days of data were lost, actual search effort was higher than indicated here.

Nomenclature

Species and common names often change as new information becomes available, and not all sources agree on what animals should be called. We have chosen the list of names published by the Society for the Study of Amphibians and Reptiles as our standard (Crother et al. 2000). This list was recently updated (Crother et al. 2003). We have included these updated names in our report so that parks will have the names most likely to be used by herpetologists in the future. When these names differ from those used in the Peterson's Field Guide series (Stebbins 2003 for the New Mexico parks; Conant and Collins 1998 for the Texas parks), we include the old names in the park species lists in parentheses.

Results

Overall Results

We documented 7,054 reptiles and amphibians at the six parks in 2003 and 6,556 reptiles and amphibians in 2004, for a total of 13,610 animals. To break these numbers down by search method, 9,596 animals were recorded during foot searches, 2,836 were incidental observations, 658 were road-cruising observations, 513 were captured in pitfall and funnel traps, and seven turtles were captured in traps.

During 2003-04, we documented 45 species at AMIS, 59 at BIBE, 46 at CAVE, 29 at FODA, 48 at GUMO, and 28 at WHSA.

We have separated the rest of the results by park. Figure 2 depicts a worker making a survey.

Figure 2. Allison Ebner records data while backpacking at GUMO. Photo by Dave Prival.

Amistad National Recreation Area

Amistad National Recreation Area, in Val Verde County, Texas, is located at the junction of three biogeographic provinces – the Chihuahuan Desert, Edwards Plateau, and Tamaulipan Thornscrub (Brown, 1994). The park covers 23,185.3 hectares (57,292 ac) and includes the lower 38.6 kilometers (24 mi) of the Devils River, the lower 22.5 kilometers (14 mi) of the Pecos River, and 119.1 kilometers (74 mi) of the Rio Grande. The park was established to manage the Amistad Reservoir, which affects or potentially could affect all of the riverways in the park, and the immediately surrounding lands up to an elevation of 348.7 meters (1,144 ft). Except for five hunt areas, most of the park lands consist of steep limestone cliffs along the river corridors. During the 2003 season, reservoir levels were lower than usual due to drought. Water elevations at the dam ranged from approximately 321.6 to 327.7 meters (1,055 to 1,075 ft) above sea level, giving us a maximum of 21.3-27.4 vertical meters (70-90 ft) of search area. The reservoir level was dramatically higher in 2004, rising to approximately 335.3 meters (1,100 ft) above sea level and significantly reducing our potential search area.

Our searches focused primarily on the shore around the eastern side of the reservoir, which is relatively accessible from roads, and the hunt areas. We conducted multiple searches at Governor's Landing, the Rock Quarry area, Evans Creek, Black Brush Point, Spur 406, the San Pedro Campground area, Long Point, Lowry Springs, Indian Wells, the area below the dam, the area on both sides of the Hwy. 277 bridge, the oak drainage northwest of the Hwy. 277 bridge, and all five hunt areas. Our survey areas outside of the eastern side of the reservoir included Pecos, Cow Creek, and Mile Canyon (near Langtry). We also conducted two 4-day canoe trips down the Devils River and two 3-day canoe trips down the Pecos River to survey along those rivers and side canyons.

Salt cedar, also known as tamarisk, has invaded some areas of the park, making those areas very difficult to survey and probably not worth the effort as far as finding herps goes. Areas that we intended to survey but decided against exploring due to the impenetrable salt cedar thickets include Pump Canyon and Seminole Canyon.

Figure 3 shows the locations of all of the reptiles and amphibians we found. The dots on the map do not indicate our total search area, because we searched several areas without finding any animals, but the map can be used to indicate roughly where we conducted surveys.

We conducted surveys at AMIS in 2003 from May 16-30 and from September 4-17, for a total of 62 person-days. Our 2004 survey period was from July 5 to September 12, for a total of 72 person-days.

During our May 2003 survey period, the park was experiencing unusually dry conditions. According to National Weather Service data, from January-April 2003, nearby Del Rio received just 4 cm (1.56 in) of rainfall, 40% of its usual precipitation for that period. May was completely dry until May 26, when the area received 0.9 cm (37 in) of rainfall, and May 27, when there was a record rainfall event that dropped 16.6 cm (6.53 in) in town.

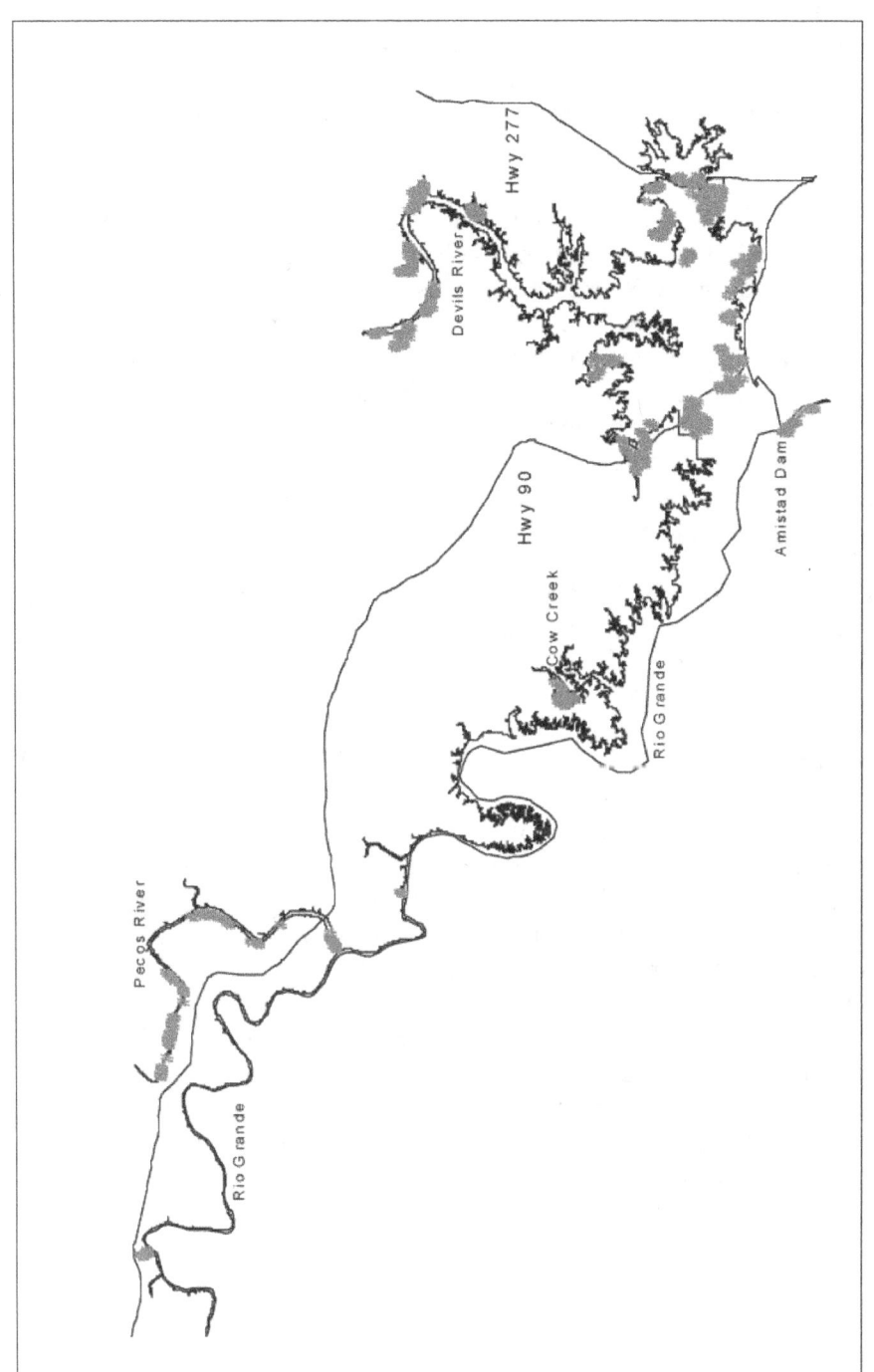

Figure 3. Locations of all reptiles and amphibians found at AMIS, 2003-04.

From June to September, rainfall was about 30% above average. Rainfall was about 25% above average between October 2003 and February 2004. Spring 2004 was especially wet, with 23.4 cm (9.21 in) of precipitation between March and May, 85% above average. From June to September, rainfall was about 20% above average.

Species List

Including the 71 animals recorded by park staff, we found 1,613 reptiles and amphibians at AMIS in 2003 and 2,261 in 2004. This totals 3,874 reptiles and amphibians representing 45 species, including nine frogs and toads, 15 lizards, 17 snakes, and four turtles (Table 2). We include Berlandier's Tortoise (*Gopherus berlandieri*) as documented even though we did not find a live animal in the park, just two scutes (small plates) from a shell.

One of these species, the Southwestern Fence Lizard (*Sceloporus cowlesi*) was just described recently. It was split off from the Eastern Fence Lizard (*Sceloporus undulatus*) based on genetic work (Leache and Reeder 2002). This species (the Southwestern Fence Lizard) is basically identical in appearance to another recently-described species, the Prairie Lizard (*Sceloporus consobrinus*). In fact, no morphological differences have been published. So, you must use range to determine which species you are looking at. AMIS is between the published range maps for the two species, so it is possible that the animals we have identified as Southwestern Fence Lizards (*Sceloporus cowlesi*) will turn out to be Prairie Lizards (*Sceloporus consobrinus*) once additional genetic work has been published.

Four of the species, the Texas Horned Lizard (*Phrynosoma cornutum*), Texas Indigo Snake (*Drymarchon melanurus erebennus*), Trans-Pecos Black-headed Snake (*Tantilla cucullata*), and Berlandier's Tortoise (*Gopherus berlandieri*) are state-threatened. We did not find any federally-listed amphibians or reptiles, nor did we expect to.

We found one non-native species, the Mediterranean House Gecko (*Hemidactylus turcicus*). This Eurasian gecko has been widely introduced, both intentionally and accidentally, into many urban areas in the southern United States. The species has apparently expanded its range into the park within the last 28 years. LoBello (1976) noted that the species had been collected in nearby Ciudad Acuña in Mexico, and there was a "possibility that it may eventually establish itself near the immediate reservoir." LoBello was correct, for we found large numbers of the species at Black Brush Point, Evans Canyon, the Devils River, and the lower Pecos River. Typically, these geckos are found on buildings where insects attracted to lights make easy prey. However, at AMIS we found them on cliff faces far from artificial illumination. Although the species is clearly invading natural areas of the park, it does not pose an obvious threat to other native species. The native gecko at AMIS, the Texas Banded Gecko (*Coleonyx brevis*), typically forages on the ground, not on the vertical walls favored by the Mediterranean House Gecko. However, the two species may compete in some more subtle way.

Table 2. Species list for Amistad National Recreation Area.
Scientific names from Conant and Collins (1998) are in parentheses.

AMPHIBIANS
ORDER ANURA – FROGS AND TOADS

Family Bufonidae – True Toads
Bufo debilis debilis – Eastern Green Toad
Bufo nebulifer – Gulf Coast Toad (*Bufo valliceps valliceps*)
Bufo punctatus – Red-spotted Toad
Bufo speciosus – Texas Toad

Family Hylidae – Treefrogs
Acris crepitans blanchardi – Blanchard's Cricket Frog

Family Leptodactylidae – Tropical Frogs
Eleutherodactylus marnockii – Cliff Chirping Frog (*Syrrhophus marnockii*)

Family Microhylidae – Narrow-mouthed Toads
Gastrophryne olivacea – Great Plains Narrow-mouthed Toad

Family Pelobatidae – Spadefoot Toads
Scaphiopus couchii – Couch's Spadefoot

Family Ranidae – True Frogs
Rana berlandieri – Rio Grande Leopard Frog (Figure 6)

REPTILES
ORDER SQUAMATA – LIZARDS AND SNAKES

Suborder Lacertilia – Lizards

Family Gekkonidae – Geckos
Coleonyx brevis – Texas Banded Gecko
Hemidactylus turcicus – Mediterranean House Gecko

Family Iguanidae – Iguanas and Allies
Cophosaurus texanus texanus – Texas Greater Earless Lizard
Crotaphytus collaris – Eastern Collared Lizard
Phrynosoma cornutum – Texas Horned Lizard
Phrynosoma modestum – Round-tailed Horned Lizard
Sceloporus cowlesi – Southwestern Fence Lizard (*Sceloporus undulatus consobrinus*)
Sceloporus merriami merriami – Merriam's Canyon Lizard
Sceloporus olivaceus – Texas Spiny Lizard
Sceloporus poinsettii poinsettii – Northern Crevice Spiny Lizard
Urosaurus ornatus schmidti – Big Bend Tree Lizard

Table 2. Species list for Amistad National Recreation Area (continued)

Family Scincidae – Skinks
Eumeces obsoletus – Great Plains Skink
Eumeces tetragrammus brevilineatus – Short-lined Skink

Family Teiidae – Whiptail Lizards
Aspidoscelis gularis gularis – Texas Spotted Whiptail (*Cnemidophorus gularis gularis*)
Aspidoscelis inornata heptagramma – Trans-Pecos Striped Whiptail (*Cnemidophorus inornatus heptagrammus*)

Suborder Serpentes – Snakes

Family Colubridae – Colubrid Snakes
Diadophis punctatus – Ring-necked Snake
Drymarchon melanurus erebennus – Texas Indigo Snake (*Drymarchon corais erebennus*)
Elaphe bairdi – Baird's Ratsnake
Hypsiglena torquata janii – Texas Nightsnake
Masticophis flagellum testaceus – Western Coachwhip
Masticophis taeniatus ornatus – Central Texas Whipsnake (*Masticophis taeniatus girardi*)
Nerodia rhombifer rhombifer – Northern Diamond-backed Watersnake
Pituophis catenifer – Gophersnake (*Pituophis melanoleucus*)
Rhinocheilus lecontei tessellatus – Texas Long-nosed Snake
Salvadora grahamiae lineata – Texas Patch-nosed Snake
Tantilla cucullata – Trans-Pecos Black-headed Snake (*Tantilla rubra cucullata/diabolica*)
Tantilla hobartsmithi – Smith's Black-headed Snake
Thamnophis proximus – Western Ribbonsnake

Family Elapidae – Coralsnakes and Allies
Micrurus tener tener – Texas Coralsnake (*Micrurus fulvius tener*)

Family Leptotyphlopidae - Threadsnakes
Leptotyphlops dulcis – Texas Threadsnake

Family Viperidae – Vipers and Pitvipers
Agkistrodon contortrix pictigaster – Trans-Pecos Copperhead
Crotalus atrox – Western Diamond-backed Rattlesnake

ORDER TESTUDINES – TURTLES

Family Emydidae – Cooters, Sliders, Box Turtles, and Allies
Pseudemys gorzugi – Rio Grande Cooter
Trachemys scripta elegans – Red-eared Slider

Table 2. Species list for Amistad National Recreation Area (continued)

Family Testudinidae – Tortoises
Gopherus berlandieri – Berlandier's Tortoise (scutes only)
Family Trionychidae – Softshell Turtles
Apalone spinifera emoryi – Texas Spiny Softshell

Species Curve

Figure 4 shows the rate at which we found species during each field season (not including park staff observations). Each season is graphed independently, so species found during 2003 are not taken into account when calculating the number of species found in 2004.

We found 35 species in 62 person-days in 2003, and 38 species in 72 person-days in 2004. It is important to note that we only have snake data for person-days 27.9 to 61 cm (11 to 24 in) 2004 because all lizard and amphibian data from that period were lost when a computer crashed. Therefore, the apparent sharp difference between the two curves during that period is probably only due to these lost data. In both years, the rate at which we found additional species began to level off after about 44 to 48 person-days.

Figure 5 shows the rate at which we found new species during our entire survey effort (not including park staff observations). After hitting a plateau at the end of the 2003 season, we had a strong start in 2004, finding six species during the first nine days that we did not find during the previous season. For the rest of the 2004 season, we found few species that we did not also find in 2003. We surveyed for a total of 134 person-days, but found no new species after 106 person-days. This species curve is not affected by the missing data from the 2004 field season.

Number of Individuals

Table 3 is a list of the number of individuals we found of each species, including park staff observations. This list serves as a rough indication of relative abundance, although it is biased toward conspicuous species and species that live in the areas we searched most often. The table indicates that we found nine species in 2004 that we did not find in 2003, and seven species in 2003 that we did not find in 2004.

Comparison of Search Methods

Most of our observations were recorded during foot searches in which we found 3,168 animals (1,313 in 2003; 1,855 in 2004) comprising 42 species (29 in 2003; 37 in 2004). We incidentally observed 532 animals (155 in 2003; 377 in 2004) comprising 26 species (20 in 2003; 18 in 2004). We captured 92 animals (67 in 2003; 25 in 2004) in pitfall traps representing nine species (6 in 2003; 7 in 2004). We observed 76 animals (71 in 2003; 5 in 2004) while road cruising comprising five species (5 in 2003; 2 in 2004). Finally, we caught seven turtles (7 in 2003; 0 in 2004) in traps representing three species.

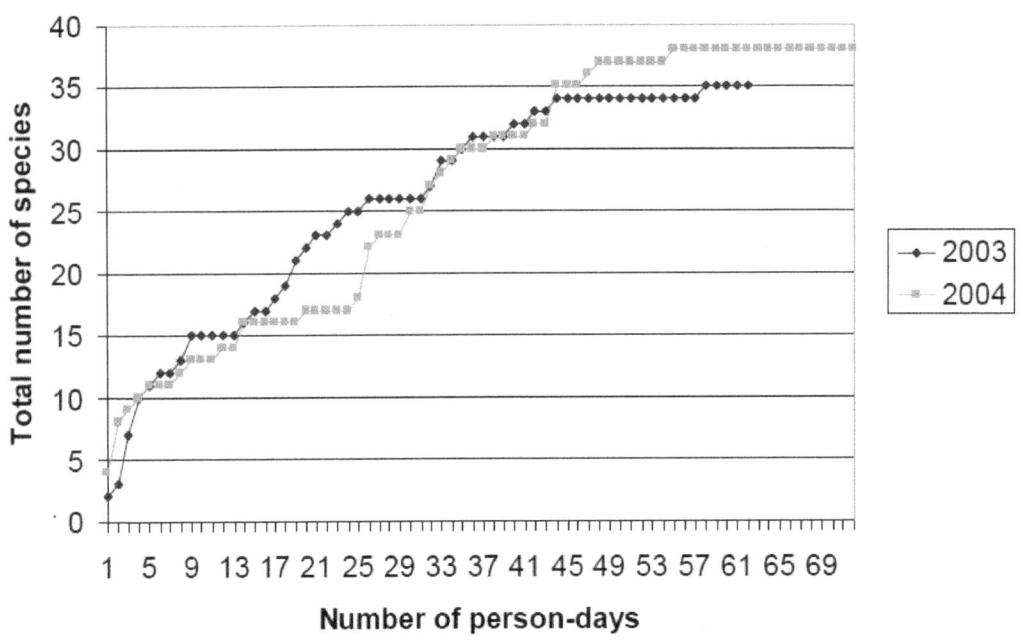

Figure 4. AMIS species curves for 2003 and 2004. This graph illustrates the rate at which we found new species during each year.

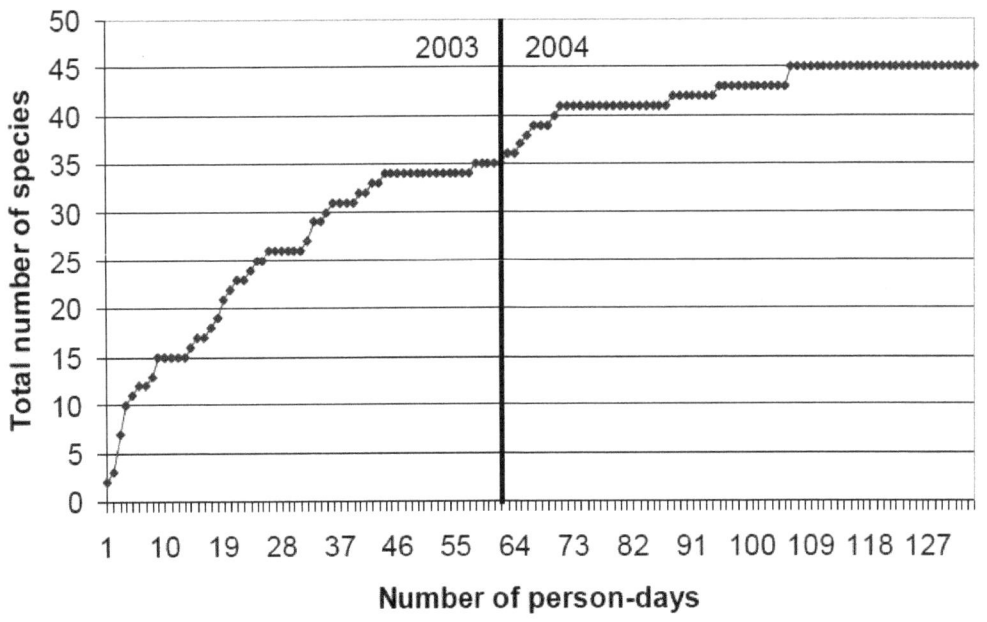

Figure 5. AMIS *species curve*: 2003-04. This graph illustrates the rate at which we found new species over the two years of the study combined.

Table 3. Number of individuals found at AMIS by species.

Species	Common Name	Number of Individuals		
		2003	2004	Total
Rana berlandieri	Rio Grande Leopard Frog (Figure 6)	201	1001	**1202**
Sceloporus merriami merriami	Merriam's Canyon Lizard	204	231	**435**
Acris crepitans blanchardi	Blanchard's Cricket Frog	279	83	**362**
Sceloporus poinsettii poinsettii	Northern Crevice Spiny Lizard	145	196	**341**
Aspidoscelis gularis gularis	Texas Spotted Whiptail	67	139	**206**
Scaphiopus couchii	Couch's Spadefoot	185	5	**190**
Eleutherodactylus marnockii	Cliff Chirping Frog	110	77	**187**
Hemidactylus turcicus	Mediterranean House Gecko	69	113	**182**
Gastrophryne olivacea	Great Plains Narrow-mouthed Toad	102	70	**172**
Cophosaurus texanus texanus	Texas Greater Earless Lizard	36	114	**150**
Bufo punctatus	Red-spotted Toad	46	67	**113**
Urosaurus ornatus schmidti	Big Bend Tree Lizard	38	24	**62**
Bufo nebulifer	Gulf Coast Toad	32	15	**47**
Sceloporus olivaceus	Texas Spiny Lizard	6	37	**43**
Bufo debilis debilis	Eastern Green Toad	31	9	**40**
Bufo speciosus	Texas Toad	12	9	**21**
Coleonyx brevis	Texas Banded Gecko	10	9	**19**
Pseudemys gorzugi	Rio Grande Cooter	4	7	**11**
Eumeces tetragrammus brevilineatus	Short-lined Skink	3	7	**10**
Masticophis flagellum testaceus	Western Coachwhip	1	8	**9**
Crotalus atrox	Western Diamond-backed Rattlesnake	1	6	**7**
Hypsiglena torquata janii	Texas Nightsnake	4	3	**7**
Thamnophis proximus	Western Ribbonsnake	2	5	**7**
Drymarchon melanurus erebennus	Texas Indigo Snake	4	2	**6**
Crotaphytus collaris	Eastern Collared Lizard	5	0	**5**
Sceloporus cowlesi	Southwestern Fence Lizard	2	3	**5**

Table 3. Number of individuals found at AMIS by species (continued).

Species	Common Name	Number of Individuals		
		2003	2004	Total
Trachemys scripta elegans	Red-eared Slider	5	0	**5**
Nerodia rhombifer rhombifer	Northern Diamond-backed Watersnake	1	3	**4**
Phrynosoma cornutum	Texas Horned Lizard	2	1	**3**
Salvadora grahamiae lineata	Texas Patch-nosed Snake	1	2	**3**
Apalone spinifera emoryi	Texas Spiny Softshell	2	0	**2**
Aspidoscelis inornata heptagramma	Trans-Pecos Striped Whiptail	1	1	**2**
Elaphe bairdi	Baird's Ratsnake	0	2	**2**
Eumeces obsoletus	Great Plains Skink	0	2	**2**
Masticophis taeniatus ornatus	Central Texas Whipsnake	0	2	**2**
Pituophis catenifer	Gophersnake	0	2	**2**
Agkistrodon contortrix pictigaster	Trans-Pecos Copperhead	1	0	**1**
Diadophis punctatus	Ring-necked Snake	1	0	**1**
Gopherus berlandieri	Berlandier's Tortoise	0	1	**1**
Micrurus tener tener	Texas Coralsnake	0	1	**1**
Phrynosoma modestum	Round-tailed Horned Lizard	0	1	**1**
Rhinocheilus lecontei tessellatus	Texas Long-nosed Snake	0	1	**1**
Tantilla cucullata	Trans-Pecos Black-headed Snake	1	0	**1**
Tantilla hobartsmithi	Smith's Black-headed Snake	1	0	**1**

Sixteen species were found during foot searches that were not documented using any other search method. These include the Trans-Pecos Copperhead (*Agkistrodon contortrix pictigaster*), Trans-Pecos Striped Whiptail (*Aspidoscelis inornata heptagramma*), Texas Banded Gecko (*Coleonyx brevis*), Western Diamond-backed Rattlesnake (*Crotalus atrox*), Texas Indigo Snake (*Drymarchon melanurus erebennus*), Baird's Ratsnake (*Elaphe bairdi*), Berlandier's Tortoise (*Gopherus berlandieri*), Texas Nightsnake (*Hypsiglena torquata janii*), Central Texas Whipsnake (*Masticophis taeniatus ornatus*), Texas Coralsnake (*Micrurus tener tener*), Round-tailed Horned Lizard (*Phrynosoma modestum*), Gophersnake (*Pituophis catenifer*), Texas Long-nosed Snake (*Rhinocheilus lecontei tessellatus*), Southwestern Fence Lizard (*Sceloporus cowlesi*), Trans-Pecos

Black-headed Snake (*Tantilla cucullata*), and Smith's Black-headed Snake (*Tantilla hobartsmithi*).

We recorded two species incidentally that were not found by any other method. These were the Ring-necked Snake (*Diadophis punctatus*) and Great Plains Skink (*Eumeces obsoletus*).

One species was only documented by the use of turtle traps and no other method, the Texas Spiny Softshell (*Apalone spinifera emoryi*).

All of the species we observed while road cruising and in pitfall traps also were found during at least one other type of survey.

Undocumented Species

According to our estimates, there are probably 10 species of reptiles and amphibians inhabiting the park that we did not find, including one lizard and nine snakes. This means that there are likely 55 species in the park in total, of which we documented 82%.

Because the park is essentially a narrow strip of land around the reservoir and rivers, it is likely that some of these species do not inhabit the park permanently but just pass through it from time to time. Furthermore, many of the records from the area are old, and because the reservoir has drastically altered virtually every aspect of the park lands (mostly in a negative way as far as herpetological diversity is concerned), many species previously present may no longer occur in the park. This, combined with the lack of previous intensive surveys in the park, means that one should not place too much confidence in our 55 species estimate.

We believe that the following species are likely to occur at AMIS, although we did not find them. This list is based on LoBello (1976), Werler and Dixon (2000), and our incomplete set of museum records.

Lizards
Aspidoscelis marmorata – Marbled Whiptail. Observed along the Rio Grande near Langtry (LoBello 1976).

Snakes
Bogertophis subocularis subocularis – Trans-Pecos Ratsnake. This species has been found frequently along Hwy. 90 near the park (Werler and Dixon 2000).

Crotalus lepidus lepidus – Mottled Rock Rattlesnake. This species was observed in 1975 outside the park by the Pecos River Bridge (LoBello 1976). There is also a voucher from the mouth of the Pecos River (TCWC 71673), although no date is given. There are several specimens from along the Pecos and Devils Rivers, dates unknown (Werler and Dixon 2000).

Crotalus molossus molossus – Northern Black-tailed Rattlesnake. This species was found in Langtry in 1975 and probably still moves into the park occasionally (LoBello 1976).

Elaphe emoryi – Great Plains Ratsnake. This species was found in the past along the Devils River (LoBello 1976), and we found this snake outside the park on Spur 406 during our survey.

Lampropeltis alterna – Gray-banded Kingsnake. This species was found under the Devils River Bridge in 1969 (LoBello 1976), and there is anecdotal evidence that it has been collected illegally within the park in recent years for sale in the black market pet trade.

Nerodia erythrogaster transversa – Blotched Watersnake. This species has been found in the past along the lower Pecos River (Werler and Dixon 2000).

Sonora semiannulata – Groundsnake. A voucher was collected south of the Hwy. 277 bridge in 1975 (LoBello 1976).

Thamnophis cyrtopsis ocellatus – Eastern Black-necked Gartersnake. Collected in the past from the lower Devils and Pecos Rivers (Werler and Dixon 2000).

Thamnophis marcianus marcianus – Marcy's Checkered Gartersnake. A voucher was collected from "Amistad Reservoir" in 1984 (TCWC 63065) and along the Devils River (Werler and Dixon 2000).

Other species that may occur at AMIS, but have never been documented in the park, include the following. We did not include these species in our estimate of the total number of species in the park.

Amphibians
Eleutherodactylus augusti latrans – Balcones Barking Frog. Known from near Langtry and Comstock (LoBello 1976).

Eurycea neotenes – Texas Salamander. Known from a 1961 record near Del Rio (LoBello 1976).

Rana catesbeiana – Bullfrog. A non-native species that was present in a stock tank near the mouth of the Devils River in the 1960s (LoBello 1976).

Spea multiplicata – Mexican Spadefoot. Known from north of Comstock and Del Rio in the 1960s (LoBello 1976).

Lizards
Aspidoscelis tessellata – Common Checkered Whiptail. Known from near Del Rio in the 1960s (LoBello 1976).

Sceloporus variabilis marmoratus – Texas Rose-bellied Lizard. There is one voucher from this species in the Texas A&M Collection from Long Point (TCWC 54501). However, given that there are no other records from Val Verde County for this species, we believe this species was probably misidentified. We don't have the date, but the specimen number indicates it was probably collected in 1977.

Snakes

Coluber constrictor oaxaca – Mexican Racer. Known from near Del Rio (Werler and Dixon 2000).

Gyalopion canum – Chihuahuan Hook-nosed Snake. This species has been found in the Comstock area (Werler and Dixon 2000).

Lampropeltis getula splendida – Desert Kingsnake. Known from the Comstock area (Werler and Dixon 2000).

Lampropeltis triangulum annulata – Mexican Milksnake. Known from near Del Rio (LoBello 1976).

Opheodrys aestivus – Rough Greensnake. Known from near Del Rio (Werler and Dixon 2000).

Tantilla nigriceps – Plains Black-headed Snake. Known from near Del Rio and near the mouth of the Pecos River (Werler and Dixon 2000).

Figure 6. Rio Grande Leopard Frog (*Rana berlandieri*) at AMIS. Photo by James Borgmeyer.

Big Bend National Park

Big Bend National Park, in Brewster County, Texas, was by far the largest park we surveyed, covering 324,219.2 hectares (801,163 ac). This immense park contains many of the vegetation types found in the Chihuahuan Desert bioregion and ranges from a low point of about 548.6 meters (1,800 ft) along the Rio Grande to a high point of about 2,377.4 meters (7,800 ft) in the Chisos Mountains. This park has received more attention from herpetologists than the other five parks in the network. Therefore, we focused most of our efforts on three mountain ranges that have been rarely visited, if visited at all, by herpetologists. These ranges were the Sierra Quemada, located just south of the Chisos Mountains; the Sierra del Caballo Muerto, located on the eastern edge of the park; and the Mesa de Anguila, located in the southwest corner of the park.

All three of these ranges are dry, exposed, rocky mountains with little or no water and are logistically challenging to survey, which explains why they had not received much attention from other herpetologists. We conducted three survey trips into the Sierra Quemada, a 5-day trip (June 2-6) and a shorter trip (August 13-15) in 2003, and a short trip (June 24-26) in 2004. We conducted one trip into the Sierra del Caballo Muerto in 2003 (August 11-13), and one in 2004 (September 1). We surveyed the Mesa de Anguila on September 21-23, 2003 and July 2, July 22, and August 14, 2004. We also conducted several short surveys into each of these ranges and surveyed other areas of the park as time permitted (mostly in 2004). We conducted 36 road cruising surveys during 2003-04.

Figure 7 shows the locations of all of the reptiles and amphibians we found. The dots on the map do not indicate our total search area, because we searched several areas without finding any animals, but the map can be used to show roughly where we conducted surveys.

In addition to the backpacking trips listed above, we conducted surveys in 2003 at BIBE on May 13-14, May 29-June 1, July 22-26, and August 6-10, for a total of 79 person-days. Our 2004 survey period was from June 23 to September 4, for a total of 52 person-days.

Species List

Including two animals recorded by park staff, we found 847 reptiles and amphibians at BIBE in 2003 and 1,412 in 2004. This totals 2,259 reptiles and amphibians representing 59 species, including nine frogs and toads, 21 lizards, 26 snakes, and three turtles (Table 4). Because Gage Dayton of Texas A&M University is completing a multi-year study of amphibians at BIBE, we focused our efforts on finding reptiles, recording amphibians only when we happened to see them. Furthermore, we did not record every amphibian we saw. We typically stopped recording frogs or toads after writing down the first ten or so if there were many of the same species in one place.

22

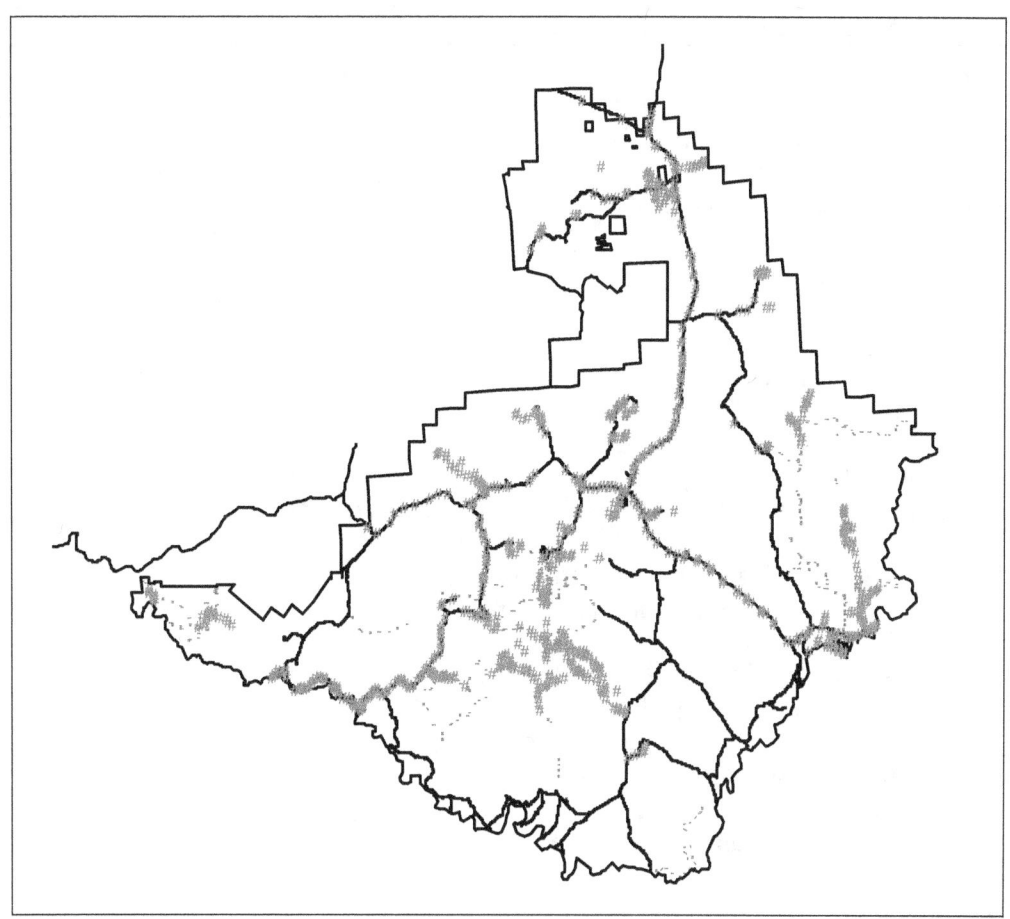

Figure 7. Locations of reptiles and amphibians found at BIBE, 2003-04

Table 4. Species list for Big Bend National Park.

AMPHIBIANS

ORDER ANURA – FROGS AND TOADS

Family Bufonidae – True Toads
Bufo debilis insidior – Western Green Toad
Bufo punctatus – Red-spotted Toad
Bufo speciosus – Texas Toad

Family Hylidae – Treefrogs
Hyla arenicolor – Canyon Treefrog

Family Leptodactylidae – Tropical Frogs
Eleutherodactylus guttilatus – Spotted Chirping Frog (*Syrrhophus guttilatus*)

Family Microhylidae – Narrow-mouthed Toads
Gastrophryne olivacea – Great Plains Narrow-mouthed Toad

Family Pelobatidae – Spadefoot Toads
Scaphiopus couchii – Couch's Spadefoot

Family Ranidae – True Frogs
Rana berlandieri – Rio Grande Leopard Frog
Rana catesbeiana – American Bullfrog

REPTILES
ORDER SQUAMATA – LIZARDS AND SNAKES

Suborder Lacertilia – Lizards

Family Anguidae – Alligator Lizards
Gerrhonotus infernalis – Texas Alligator Lizard (*Gerrhonotus liocephalis infernalis*)

Family Gekkonidae – Geckos
Coleonyx brevis – Texas Banded Gecko
Coleonyx reticulatus – Reticulate Banded Gecko
Hemidactylus turcicus – Mediterranean House Gecko

Family Iguanidae – Iguanas and Allies
Cophosaurus texanus scitulus – Chihuahuan Greater Earless Lizard
Crotaphytus collaris – Eastern Collared Lizard
Gambelia wislizenii – Long-nosed Leopard Lizard
Phrynosoma cornutum – Texas Horned Lizard
Phrynosoma modestum – Round-tailed Horned Lizard
Sceloporus cowlesi – Southwestern Fence Lizard (*Sceloporus undulatus consobrinus*)

Table 4. Species list for Big Bend National Park (continued).

Sceloporus magister bimaculosus – Twin-spotted Spiny Lizard
Sceloporus merriami annulatus – Big Bend Canyon Lizard
Sceloporus poinsettii poinsettii – Northern Crevice Spiny Lizard
Urosaurus ornatus schmidti – Big Bend Tree Lizard
Uta stansburiana – Common Side-blotched Lizard

Family Scincidae – Skinks
Eumeces obsoletus – Great Plains Skink
Eumeces tetragrammus brevilineatus – Short-lined Skink

Family Teiidae – Whiptail Lizards
Aspidoscelis inornata heptagramma – Trans-Pecos Striped Whiptail (*Cnemidophorus inornatus heptagrammus*)
Aspidoscelis marmorata – Marbled Whiptail (*Cnemidophorus marmoratus*)
Aspidoscelis septemvittata septemvittata – Big Bend Spotted Whiptail (*Cnemidophorus septemvittatus septemvittatus*)
Aspidoscelis tesselata – Common Checkered Whiptail (*Cnemidophorus tesselatus*)

Suborder Serpentes – Snakes

Family Colubridae – Colubrid Snakes
Arizona elegans elegans – Kansas Glossy Snake
Bogertophis subocularis subocularis – Trans-Pecos Ratsnake
Diadophis punctatus – Ring-necked Snake
Elaphe bairdi – Baird's Ratsnake
Elaphe emoryi - Great Plains Ratsnake (*Elaphe guttata emoryi*)
Gyalopion canum – Chihuahuan Hook-nosed Snake
Hypsiglena torquata janii – Texas Nightsnake
Masticophis flagellum testaceus – Western Coachwhip
Masticophis taeniatus ornatus – Central Texas Whipsnake (*Masticophis taeniatus girardi*)
Nerodia erythrogaster transversa – Blotched Watersnake
Pituophis catenifer affinis – Sonoran Gophersnake (*Pituophis melanoleucus affinis*)
Rhinocheilus lecontei tessellatus – Texas Long-nosed Snake
Salvadora grahamiae grahamiae – Mountain Patch-nosed Snake
Salvadora hexalepis deserticola – Big Bend Patch-nosed Snake (*Salvadora deserticola*)
Sonora semiannulata semiannulata – Variable Groundsnake
Tantilla cucullata – Trans-Pecos Black-headed Snake (*Tantilla rubra cucullata/ diabolica*)
Tantilla hobartsmithi – Smith's Black-headed Snake
Thamnophis cyrtopsis cyrtopsis – Western Black-necked Gartersnake
Thamnophis marcianus marcianus – Marcy's Checkered Gartersnake
Trimorphodon biscutatus vilkinsonii – Texas Lyresnake

Table 4. Species list for Big Bend National Park (continued).

Family Leptotyphlopidae - Threadsnakes
Leptotyphlops humilis segregus – Trans-Pecos Threadsnake

Family Viperidae – Vipers and Pitvipers
Agkistrodon contortrix pictigaster – Trans-Pecos Copperhead
Crotalus atrox – Western Diamond-backed Rattlesnake
Crotalus lepidus lepidus – Mottled Rock Rattlesnake (Figure 10)
Crotalus molossus molossus – Northern Black-tailed Rattlesnake
Crotalus scutulatus scutulatus – Northern Mohave Rattlesnake

ORDER TESTUDINES – TURTLES

Family Emydidae – Cooters, Sliders, Box Turtles, and Allies
Trachemys gaigeae gaigeae – Big Bend Slider

Family Kinosternidae – Mud Turtles
Kinosternon flavescens – Yellow Mud Turtle

Family Trionychidae – Softshell Turtles
Apalone spinifera emoryi – Texas Spiny Softshell

Four of the species, the Texas Horned Lizard (*Phrynosoma cornutum*), Reticulate Banded Gecko (*Coleonyx reticulatus*), Trans-Pecos Black-headed Snake (*Tantilla cucullata*), and Texas Lyresnake (*Trimorphodon biscutatus vilkinsonii*), are state-threatened. We did not find any federally-listed amphibians or reptiles.

We found two non-native species, the Mediterranean House Gecko (*Hemidactylus turcicus*) and American Bullfrog (*Rana catesbeiana*). The Mediterranean House Gecko, a Eurasian species, has been widely introduced, both intentionally and accidentally, in many urban areas in the southern United States. Typically, these geckos are found on buildings where insects attracted to lights make easy prey. We found it on the walls of Barker House (near Rio Grande Village), at Rio Grande Village, and at Panther Junction. Unlike at AMIS, this species apparently has not invaded natural areas at BIBE. One native gecko at BIBE, the Texas Banded Gecko (*Coleonyx brevis*), typically forages on the ground, not on the vertical walls favored by the Mediterranean House Gecko. However, the two species may compete in some more subtle way. The other native gecko at BIBE, the Reticulate Banded Gecko (*Coleonyx reticulatus*), prefers cliff crevices, so there may be direct competition if the Mediterranean House Gecko invades natural areas in the future.

We heard American Bullfrogs (*Rana catesbeiana*) calling from the Mexican side of Santa Elena Canyon and found them in the park at Rio Grande Village. This highly invasive species, native to the Eastern United States, was intentionally introduced to western states by state wildlife agencies during the 20th century. Due to their apparently huge appetites, generalist diet, and large adult body size, these frogs have become a severe threat to many native species, in particular leopard frogs and gartersnakes.

Because our surveys of the Sierra Quemada, Sierra del Caballo Muerto, and Mesa de Anguila are of particular interest to the park, we list the species we found in each of these ranges below (Tables 5, 6, and 7).

Table 5. Species found in the Sierra Quemada.

AMPHIBIANS
ORDER ANURA – FROGS AND TOADS

Family Bufonidae – True Toads
Bufo punctatus – Red-spotted Toad

Familiy Hylidae - Treefrogs
Hyla arenicolor – Canyon Treefrog

Family Leptodactylidae – Tropical Frogs
Eleutherodactylus guttilatus – Spotted Chirping Frog

Family Microhylidae – Narrow-mouthed Toads
Gastrophryne olivacea – Great Plains Narrow-mouthed Toad

Family Ranidae – True Frogs
Rana berlandieri – Rio Grande Leopard Frog

REPTILES
ORDER SQUAMATA – LIZARDS AND SNAKES

Suborder Lacertilia – Lizards

Family Gekkonidae – Geckos
Coleonyx brevis – Texas Banded Gecko

Family Iguanidae – Iguanas and Allies
Cophosaurus texanus scitulus – Chihuahuan Greater Earless Lizard
Sceloporus cowlesi – Southwestern Fence Lizard
Sceloporus merriami annulatus – Big Bend Canyon Lizard
Sceloporus poinsettii poinsettii – Northern Crevice Spiny Lizard
Urosaurus ornatus schmidti – Big Bend Tree Lizard
Uta stansburiana – Common Side-blotched Lizard

Family Scincidae – Skinks
Eumeces obsoletus – Great Plains Skink

Family Teiidae – Whiptail Lizards
Aspidoscelis marmorata – Marbled Whiptail
Aspidoscelis septemvittata septemvittata – Big Bend Spotted Whiptail

Table 5. Species found in the Sierra Quemada (continued).

Suborder Serpentes – Snakes

Family Colubridae – Colubrid Snakes
Gyalopion canum – Chihuahuan Hook-nosed Snake
Hypsiglena torquata janii – Texas Nightsnake
Masticophis flagellum testaceus – Western Coachwhip
Masticophis taeniatus ornatus – Central Texas Whipsnake
Salvadora grahamiae grahamiae – Mountain Patch-nosed Snake
Salvadora hexalepis deserticola – Big Bend Patch-nosed Snake
Tantilla hobartsmithi – Smith's Black-headed Snake
Thamnophis cyrtopsis cyrtopsis – Western Black-necked Gartersnake

Family Viperidae – Vipers and Pitvipers
Crotalus atrox – Western Diamond-backed Rattlesnake

Table 5. Species found in the Sierra del Caballo Muerto.

AMPHIBIANS
ORDER ANURA – FROGS AND TOADS

Family Bufonidae – True Toads
Bufo punctatus – Red-spotted Toad

REPTILES
ORDER SQUAMATA – LIZARDS AND SNAKES

Suborder Lacertilia – Lizards

Family Gekkonidae – Geckos
Coleonyx brevis – Texas Banded Gecko
Coleonyx reticulatus – Reticulate Banded Gecko

Family Iguanidae – Iguanas and Allies
Cophosaurus texanus scitulus – Chihuahuan Greater Earless Lizard
Sceloporus cowlesi – Southwestern Fence Lizard
Sceloporus merriami annulatus – Big Bend Canyon Lizard
Sceloporus poinsettii poinsettii – Northern Crevice Spiny Lizard
Urosaurus ornatus schmidti – Common Side-blotched Lizard

Family Scincidae – Skinks
Eumeces obsoletus – Great Plains Skink
Eumeces tetragrammus brevilineatus – Short-lined Skink

Family Teiidae – Whiptail Lizards
Aspidoscelis inornata heptagramma – Trans-Pecos Striped Whiptail
Aspidoscelis marmorata – Marbled Whiptail

Table 6. Species found in the Sierra del Caballo Muerto (continued).

Aspidoscelis septemvittata septemvittata – Big Bend Spotted Whiptail

Suborder Serpentes – Snakes

Family Colubridae – Colubrid Snakes
Bogertophis subocularis subocularis – Trans-Pecos Ratsnake
Diadophis punctatus – Ring-necked Snake
Gyalopion canum – Chihuahuan Hook-nosed Snake
Hypsiglena torquata janii – Texas Nightsnake
Rhinocheilus lecontei tessellatus – Texas Long-nosed Snake
Salvadora grahamiae grahamiae – Mountain Patch-nosed Snake
Sonora semiannulata semiannulata – Variable Groundsnake
Tantilla hobartsmithi – Smith's Black-headed Snake
Trimorphodon biscutatus vilkinsonii – Texas Lyresnake

Family Viperidae – Vipers and Pitvipers
Crotalus lepidus lepidus – Mottled Rock Rattlesnake (Figure 10)
Crotalus molossus molossus – Northern Black-tailed Rattlesnake

Table 6. Species found on Mesa de Anguila.

REPTILES

ORDER SQUAMATA – LIZARDS AND SNAKES

Suborder Lacertilia – Lizards

Family Gekkonidae – Geckos
Coleonyx brevis – Texas Banded Gecko
Coleonyx reticulatus – Reticulate Banded Gecko

Family Iguanidae – Iguanas and Allies
Cophosaurus texanus scitulus – Chihuahuan Greater Earless Lizard
Sceloporus merriami annulatus – Big Bend Canyon Lizard
Urosaurus ornatus schmidti – Big Bend Tree Lizard

Family Teiidae – Whiptail Lizards
Aspidoscelis inornata heptagramma – Trans-Pecos Striped Whiptail
Aspidoscelis marmorata – Marbled Whiptail
Aspidoscelis septemvittata septemvittata – Big Bend Spotted Whiptail
Aspidoscelis tesselata – Common Checkered Whiptail

Suborder Serpentes – Snakes

Family Colubridae – Colubrid Snakes
Hypsiglena torquata janii – Texas Nightsnake
Rhinocheilus lecontei tessellatus – Texas Long-nosed Snake

Table 7. Species found on Mesa de Anguila (continued).

Family Viperidae – Vipers and Pitvipers
Crotalus atrox – Western Diamond-backed Rattlesnake
Crotalus molossus molossus – Northern Black-tailed Rattlesnake

Species Curves

Figure 8 shows the rate at which we found new species during our surveys (not including park staff observations). Each season is graphed independently, so species found during 2003 are not taken into account when calculating the number of species found in 2004.

We found 43 species in 79 person-days in 2003, and 54 species in 52 person-days in 2004. In 2003, we primarily focused our efforts on the three dry mountain ranges mentioned above. In 2004, our search effort encompassed different areas of the park, partially explaining the much higher rate at which we found new species that year. In both years, the rate at which we found additional species began to level off after about 39 to 41 person-days.

Figure 9 shows the rate at which we found new species during our entire survey effort. Again, park staff observations are not included. We found the first 24 species within 16 days. After that, the rate at which we found new species declined. However, we continued to find new species during the entire course of the survey, never reaching a real plateau.

Number of Individuals

Table 7 is a list of the number of individuals we found of each species. This list serves as a rough indication of relative abundance, although it is biased toward conspicuous species and species that live in the areas we searched most often. The table shows that we found 15 species in 2004 that we did not find in 2003, and three species in 2003 that we did not find in 2004.

Comparison of Search Methods

Most of our observations were recorded during foot searches, during which we found 1,008 animals (563 in 2003; 445 in 2004) comprising 48 species (31 in 2003; 39 in 2004). We incidentally observed 817 animals (229 in 2003; 588 in 2004) comprising 49 species (32 in 2003; 45 in 2004). We observed 434 animals (55 in 2003; 379 in 2004) while road cruising comprising 25 species (15 in 2003; 24 in 2004).

Eight species were found during foot searches that were not documented using any other search method. These include the Reticulate Banded Gecko (*Coleonyx reticulatus*), Spotted Chirping Frog (*Eleutherodactylus guttilatus*), Chihuahuan Hook-nosed Snake (*Gyalopion canum*), Trans-Pecos Threadsnake (*Leptotyphlops humilis segregus*), Texas Horned Lizard (*Phrynosoma cornutum*), Mountain Patch-nosed Snake (*Salvadora grahamiae grahamiae*), Trans-Pecos Black-headed Snake (*Tantilla cucullata*), and Texas Lyresnake (*Trimorphodon biscutatus vilkinsonii*).

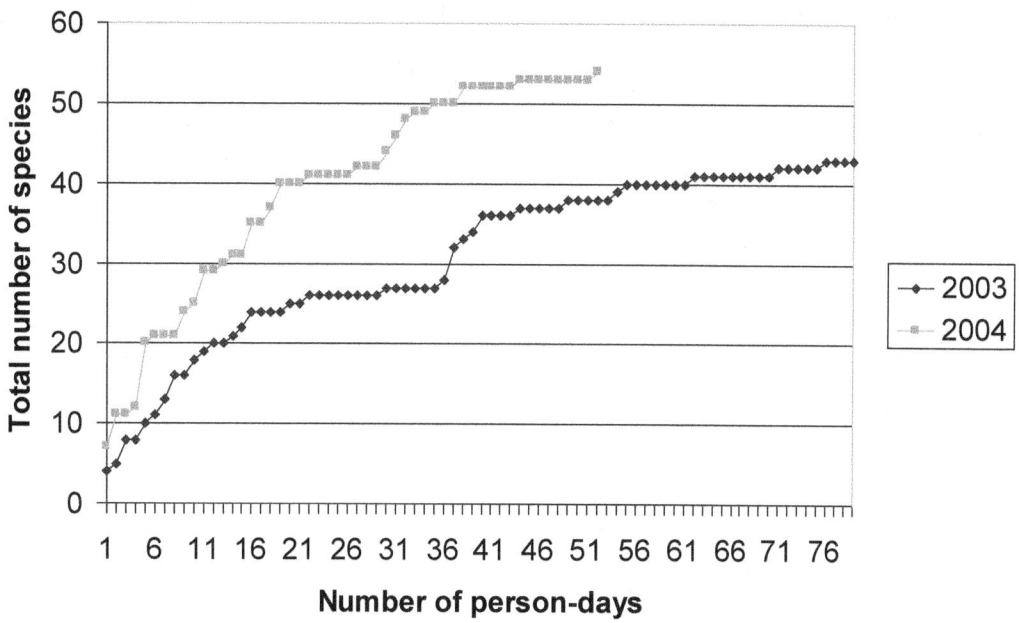

Figure 8. BIBE species curves for 2003 and 2004. This graph illustrates the rate at which we found new species each year.

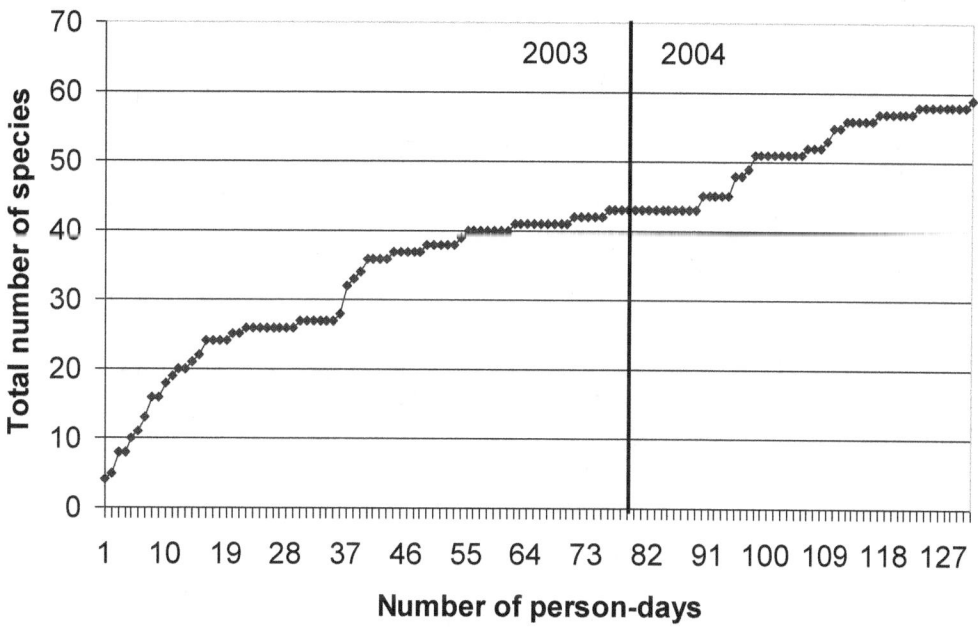

Figure 9. BIBE species curve: 2003-04. This graph illustrates the rate at which we found new species over the two years of the study combined.

Table 7. Number of individuals found at BIBE by species.

Species	Common Name	Number of Individuals		
		2003	2004	Total
Sceloporus merriami annulatus	Big Bend Canyon Lizard	222	186	**408**
Rana berlandieri	Rio Grande Leopard Frog	153	95	**248**
Cophosaurus texanus scitulus	Chihuahuan Greater Earless Lizard	96	82	**178**
Aspidoscelis marmorata	Marbled Whiptail	35	149	**184**
Bufo punctatus	Red-spotted Toad	32	121	**153**
Bufo speciosus	Texas Toad	5	126	**131**
Aspidoscelis septemvittata septemvittata	Big Bend Spotted Whiptail	53	63	**116**
Crotalus atrox	Western Diamond-backed Rattlesnake	29	57	**86**
Scaphiopus couchii	Couch's Spadefoot	6	64	**70**
Sceloporus poinsettii poinsettii	Northern Crevice Spiny Lizard	20	47	**67**
Urosaurus ornatus schmidti	Big Bend Tree Lizard	31	36	**67**
Uta stansburiana	Common Side-blotched Lizard	7	45	**52**
Hyla arenicolor	Canyon Treefrog	17	25	**42**
Coleonyx brevis	Texas Banded Gecko	14	24	**38**
Thamnophis cyrtopsis cyrtopsis	Western Black-necked Gartersnake	17	18	**35**
Aspidoscelis inornata heptagramma	Trans-Pecos Striped Whiptail	18	16	**34**
Masticophis flagellum testaceus	Western Coachwhip	8	22	**30**
Hypsiglena torquata janii	Texas Nightsnake	9	19	**28**
Crotalus molossus molossus	Northern Black-tailed Rattlesnake	8	19	**27**
Kinosternon flavescens	Yellow Mud Turtle	1	23	**24**
Bogertophis subocularis subocularis	Trans-Pecos Ratsnake	10	13	**23**
Gastrophryne olivacea	Great Plains Narrow-mouthed Toad	1	19	**20**
Bufo debilis insidior	Western Green Toad	0	18	**18**
Sceloporus cowlesi	Southwestern Fence Lizard	4	10	**14**
Hemidactylus turcicus	Mediterranean House Gecko	8	5	**13**
Rhinocheilus lecontei tessellatus	Texas Long-nosed Snake	6	6	**12**
Crotalus scutulatus	Mohave Rattlesnake	4	7	**11**
Sceloporus magister bimaculosus	Twin-spotted Spiny Lizard	0	10	**10**

Table 8. Number of individuals found at BIBE by species (continued).

Species	Common Name	Number of Individuals		
		2003	2004	Total
Phrynosoma modestum	Round-tailed Horned Lizard	1	8	**9**
Eumeces obsoletus	Great Plains Skink	3	5	**8**
Eumeces tetragrammus brevilineatus	Short-lined Skink	0	8	**8**
Sonora semiannulata semiannulata	Variable Groundsnake	2	6	**8**
Apalone spinifera emoryi	Texas Spiny Softshell	0	7	**7**
Arizona elegans elegans	Kansas Glossy Snake	0	7	**7**
Crotaphytus collaris	Eastern Collared Lizard	3	3	**6**
Masticophis taeniatus ornatus	Central Texas Whipsnake	3	3	**6**
Pituophis catenifer affinis	Sonoran Gophersnake	2	4	**6**
Agkistrodon contortrix pictigaster	Trans-Pecos Copperhead	4	0	**4**
Rana catesbeiana	American Bullfrog	0	4	**4**
Tantilla hobartsmithi	Smith's Black-headed Snake	1	3	**4**
Thamnophis marcianus marcianus	Marcy's Checkered Gartersnake	0	4	**4**
Trachemys gaigeae gaigeae	Big Bend Slider	0	4	**4**
Aspidoscelis tesselata	Common Checkered Whiptail	1	2	**3**
Coleonyx reticulatus	Reticulate Banded Gecko (Figure 10)	0	3	**3**
Crotalus lepidus lepidus	Mottled Rock Rattlesnake	2	1	**3**
Diadophis punctatus	Ring-necked Snake	1	2	**3**
Eleutherodactylus guttilatus	Spotted Chirping Frog	3	0	**3**
Gerrhonotus infernalis	Texas Alligator Lizard	1	2	**3**
Elaphe bairdi	Baird's Ratsnake	0	2	**2**
Gambelia wislizenii	Long-nosed Leopard Lizard	0	2	**2**
Gyalopion canum	Chihuahuan Hook-nosed Snake	2	0	**2**
Nerodia erythrogaster transversa	Blotched Watersnake	0	2	**2**
Salvadora grahamiae grahamiae	Mountain Patch-nosed Snake	1	1	**2**
Salvadora hexalepis deserticola	Big Bend Patch-nosed Snake	1	1	**2**
Elaphe emoryi	Great Plains Ratsnake	0	1	**1**
Leptotyphlops humilis segregus	Trans-Pecos Threadsnake	1	0	**1**
Phrynosoma cornutum	Texas Horned Lizard	0	1	**1**
Tantilla cucullata	Trans-Pecos Black-headed Snake	0	1	**1**

Table 8. Number of individuals found at BIBE by species (continued).

Species	Common Name	Number of Individuals		
		2003	2004	Total
Trimorphodon biscutatus vilkinsonii	Texas Lyresnake	1	0	1

We recorded six species incidentally that were not found by any other method. These were the Texas Spiny Softshell (*Apalone spinifera emoryi*), Common Checkered Whiptail (*Aspidoscelis tesselata*), Eastern Collared Lizard (*Crotaphytus collaris*), American Bullfrog (*Rana catesbeiana*), Big Bend Patch-nosed Snake (*Salvadora hexalepis deserticola*), and Big Bend Slider (*Trachemys gaigeae gaigeae*).

We found one species by road cruising and no other method – the Great Plains Ratsnake (*Elaphe emoryi*).

Undocumented Species
According to the BIBE Amphibians and Reptiles Checklist (Dayton 2002), there are probably 69 species in the park at present. Although our primary goal at BIBE was to survey the three mountain ranges we visited, rather than conduct a complete inventory of the park, we still wanted to document as many of the park's species as possible.

According to the list, ten species occur in the park that we did not find, including one toad, one salamander, one lizard, four snakes, and three turtles. In total, assuming that the park list is correct, we documented 86% of the park's reptiles and amphibians. It is difficult to estimate the percentage of species we found in the three mountain ranges we surveyed due to the lack of previous surveys in the ranges.

The following list contains species that probably occur in the park, but that we did not find this year. Locality data is taken from Dayton (2002).

Amphibians
Frogs and Toads

Spea multiplicata – Mexican Spadefoot. Collected in 1990 from the Rosillos Mountains (SRSU 1355). Reportedly found in the past at Panther Junction as well.

Salamanders

Ambystoma tigrinum mavortium – Barred Tiger Salamander. Has been found near Panther Junction, but unknown whether these animals naturally inhabit the area or were released pets.

Lizards

Anolis carolinensis – Green Anole. A non-native species that has been introduced at Rio Grande Village.

Lampropeltis alterna – Gray-banded Kingsnake. Found in the Chisos Mountains and foothills.

Lampropeltis getula splendida – Desert Kingsnake. Found in lower elevations of the park.

Lampropeltis triangulum – Milksnake. Found in the Chisos Mountains and foothills, as well as in floodplains on the east side of the park.

Leptotyphlops dissectus – New Mexico Threadsnake. Inhabits the Chisos Mountains.

Turtles

Gopherus berlandieri – Berlandier's Tortoise. A species that is not native to the park, but has been found in the Chisos Basin and Rio Grande Village, probably because park visitors have released them there as unwanted pets.

Terrapene ornata luteola – Desert Box Turtle. Known from Panther Junction and near Persimmon Gap.

Trachemys scripta elegans – Red-eared Slider. A non-native species found along the Rio Grande.

According to the BIBE Amphibians and Reptiles Checklist (Dayton 2002), the following species used to occur in the park but may have been extirpated in recent years; their occurrence in the park has not been documented though they may occur there.

Amphibians

Frogs and Toads

Bufo woodhousii australis – Southwestern Woodhouse's Toad. Last seen in the Rio Grande floodplain in the early 1970s.

Hyla cinerea – Green Treefrog. Not native to the area, but has been heard calling at Rio Grande Village.

Reptiles

Snakes

Crotalus viridis viridis – Prairie Rattlesnake. May occur in the northern part of the park.

Heterodon nasicus kennerlyi – Mexican Hog-nosed Snake. One record from Panther Junction.

Tantilla nigriceps – Plains Black-headed Snake. Possibly occurs in the Basin or Rio Grande Village. Note that this species is very similar in appearance to *Tantilla hobartsmithi*, Smith's Black-headed Snake, which definitely occurs in the park.

Figure 10. Reticulate Banded Gecko (*Coleonyx reticulatus*) at BIBE. Photo by Ian Murray.

Carlsbad Caverns National Park

Carlsbad Caverns National Park, in Eddy County, New Mexico, includes 18,925.5 hectares (46,766 ac) of steep limestone hills and canyons in addition to the caves for which it was established. Ranging from 1,095.8 to 1,987.3 meters (3,595 to 6,520 ft) elevation, this park has little permanent water except at Rattlesnake Spring. The Rattlesnake Spring unit is located near the Black River and is not continuous with the rest of the park.

At CAVE, our efforts were supplemented by Mike Woolman in 2003 and Chris Newsom in 2004, who have written separate reports. The areas we surveyed in 2003 include the sewage disposal pond area, Rattlesnake Springs, Bat Cave Draw, Bear Canyon, the Slaughter Canyon drainage and the low area near the mouth of Slaughter Canyon, Double Canyon and other canyons in the southwest corner of the park, Grammar Seep, Kirkland and Putman Canyons and other canyons in the northwest corner of the park, Lechuguilla Canyon, the Rattlesnake Canyon drainage, Walnut Canyon, portions of the Guadalupe Ridge Road, and the area above Yucca Canyon.

Figure 11 shows the locations of all of the reptiles and amphibians we found. Data collected by Mike Woolman and Chris Newsom are included in this map. The dots on the map do not indicate our total search area, because we searched several areas without finding any animals, but the map can be used to show roughly where we conducted surveys.

In 2003, we conducted surveys at CAVE on May 7-8, June 23-27, July 7-10, July 28-August 1, and August 27-29 for a total of 67 person-days. Mike Woolman was stationed at the park from May 15 to September 23 and conducted surveys most days. In 2004, Dave Prival conducted surveys at CAVE on July 1, July 12-13, and August 19-21. Chris Newsom was stationed at the park from June 3 to August 19.

According to the National Weather Service, Carlsbad, NM, received well below normal levels of precipitation during Spring and Summer 2003. From June-September only 4.4 cm (1.74 in) of rain fell, 75% below normal. According to Mike Woolman, the park received even less precipitation than the town from May-September. As a result, 2003 was not a good year in which to conduct a reptile and amphibian inventory at CAVE. We never heard any amphibians calling from within the park, and it seems likely that some frog and toad species simply remained underground all year due to the lack of monsoon rains. Snake activity is also typically correlated with rainfall.

In contrast, 2004 was a very wet year. Table 8 displays the differences in rainfall between years. Between March and September 2004, Carlsbad received over 4.5 times as much precipitation as during the same period in 2003.

37

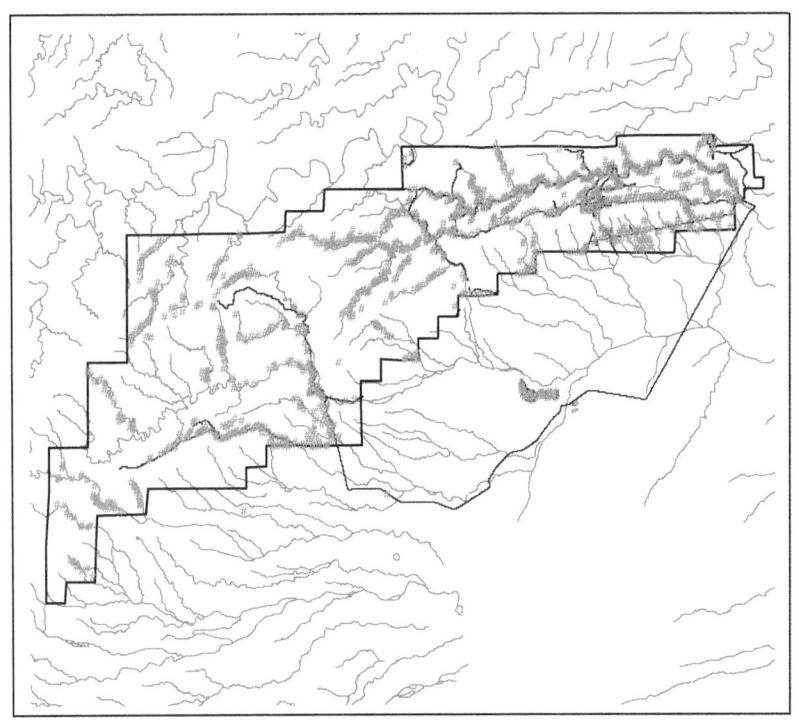

Figure 11. Locations of reptiles and amphibians found at CAVE, 2003-04.

Table 8. Monthly precipitation (in inches) in Carlsbad, NM.
Data from National Weather Service.

	2003	2004
March	0.22	1.69
April	0.00	4.01
May	1.73	0.36
June	0.14	3.09
July	0.78	3.22
August	0.29	0.66
September	0.53	3.63
TOTAL	**3.69**	**16.66**

Species List

Including the 1,583 animals recorded by Mike Woolman, the 544 animals recorded by Chris Newsom, and the 636 animals recorded by park staff, we found 2,284 reptiles and amphibians at CAVE in 2003 and 1,291 in 2004. This totals 3,575 reptiles and amphibians representing 46 species, including eight frogs and toads, 15 lizards, 20 snakes, and three turtles (Table 9).

We found one state-endangered species, the Gray-banded Kingsnake (*Lampropeltis alterna*), and two state-threatened species, the Mottled Rock Rattlesnake (*Crotalus lepidus lepidus*) and the Rio Grande Cooter (*Pseudemys gorzugi*). We did not find any federally-listed amphibians or reptiles.

We found one non-native species, the American Bullfrog (*Rana catesbeiana*). This highly invasive species, native to the Eastern United States, was intentionally introduced to western states by state wildlife agencies during the 20th century. Due to their apparently huge appetites, generalist diet, and large adult body size, these frogs have become a severe threat to many native species, in particular leopard frogs and gartersnakes. We only found these frogs in Rattlesnake Spring. We removed three of them, but there is still at least one very large American Bullfrog in the spring, perhaps more.

Table 9. Species list for Carlsbad Caverns National Park.
Scientific names from Stebbins (2003) are in parentheses.

AMPHIBIANS
ORDER ANURA – FROGS AND TOADS

Family Bufonidae – True Toads
Bufo cognatus – Great Plains Toad
Bufo debilis insidior – Western Green Toad
Bufo punctatus – Red-spotted Toad
Bufo speciosus – Texas Toad

Family Pelobatidae – Spadefoot Toads
Scaphiopus couchii – Couch's Spadefoot
Spea multiplicata – Mexican Spadefoot

Family Ranidae – True Frogs
Rana berlandieri – Rio Grande Leopard Frog
Rana catesbeiana – American Bullfrog

REPTILES
ORDER SQUAMATA – LIZARDS AND SNAKES

Suborder Lacertilia – Lizards

Family Gekkonidae – Geckos
Coleonyx brevis – Texas Banded Gecko

Table 10. Species list for Carlsbad Caverns National Park (continued).

Family Iguanidae – Iguanas and Allies
Cophosaurus texanus scitulus - Chihuahuan Greater Earless Lizard
Crotaphytus collaris – Eastern Collared Lizard
Phrynosoma cornutum – Texas Horned Lizard
Phrynosoma modestum – Round-tailed Horned Lizard
Sceloporus cowlesi – Southwestern Fence Lizard (*Sceloporus undulatus consobrinus*)
Sceloporus poinsettii poinsettii – Northern Crevice Spiny Lizard
Urosaurus ornatus schmidti – Big Bend Tree Lizard
Uta stansburiana – Common Side-blotched Lizard

Family Scincidae – Skinks
Eumeces multivirgatus epipleurotus – Variable Skink
Eumeces obsoletus – Great Plains Skink

Family Teiidae – Whiptail Lizards
Aspidoscelis exsanguis – Chihuahuan Spotted Whiptail (*Cnemidophorus exsanguis*)
Aspidoscelis gularis gularis – Texas Spotted Whiptail (*Cnemidophorus gularis*)
Aspidoscelis inornata heptagramma – Trans-Pecos Striped Whiptail (*Cnemidophorus inornatus*)
Aspidoscelis tesselata – Common Checkered Whiptail (*Cnemidophorus tesselatus*)

Suborder Serpentes – Snakes

Family Colubridae – Colubrid Snakes
Bogertophis subocularis subocularis – Trans-Pecos Ratsnake
Diadophis punctatus – Ring-necked Snake
Elaphe emoryi – Great Plains Ratsnake (*Elaphe guttata emoryi*)
Gyalopion canum – Chihuahuan Hook-nosed Snake
Heterodon nasicus kennerlyi – Mexican Hog-nosed Snake
Hypsiglena torquata janii – Texas Nightsnake
Lampropeltis alterna – Gray-banded Kingsnake
Masticophis flagellum testaceus – Western Coachwhip
Masticophis taeniatus – Striped Whipsnake
Pituophis catenifer affinis – Sonoran Gophersnake
Rhinocheilus lecontei tessellatus – Texas Long-nosed Snake
Salvadora grahamiae grahamiae – Mountain Patch-nosed Snake
Sonora semiannnulata semiannulata – Variable Groundsnake
Tantilla hobartsmithi – Smith's Black-headed Snake
Thamnophis cyrtopsis cyrtopsis – Western Black-necked Gartersnake
Thamnophis marcianus marcianus – Marcy's Checkered Gartersnake

Family Leptotyphlopidae - Threadsnakes
Leptotyphlops dissectus – New Mexico Threadsnake (*Leptotyphlops dulcis*)

Table 10. Species list for Carlsbad Caverns National Park (continued).

Family Viperidae – Vipers and Pitvipers
Crotalus atrox – Western Diamond-backed Rattlesnake
Crotalus lepidus lepidus – Mottled Rock Rattlesnake
Crotalus molossus molossus – Northern Black-tailed Rattlesnake

ORDER TESTUDINES – TURTLES

Family Emydidae – Cooters, Sliders, Box Turtles, and Allies
Pseudemys gorzugi – Rio Grande Cooter
Terrapene ornata ornata – Ornate Box Turtle

Family Kinosternidae – Mud Turtles
Kinosternon flavescens – Yellow Mud Turtle

Species Curve

Figure 12 shows the rate at which we found new species during our surveys. Park staff observations are not included, but data collected by park-supported technicians are included. Each season is graphed independently, so species found during 2003 are not taken into account when calculating the number of species found in 2004.

We found 40 species in 157 person-days in 2003, and 44 species in 54 person-days in 2004. The rate at which we found species was similar during both years for the first 30 person-days. Each year, we found 35 species within the first 30 person-days. However, the rate at which we found new species tailed off considerably after the first 30 person-days in 2003, whereas we continued to find new species at approximately the same rate in 2004 throughout the season. Increased herp activity due to the wetter weather in 2004 may explain why we continued to find new species throughout the season that year.

Figure 13 shows the rate at which we found new species during our entire survey effort. Again, park staff observations are not included, but data collected by park-supported technicians are included. As noted above, we found the first 35 species within 30 person-days. After that, the rate at which we found new species declined. However, we found new species at a moderate rate in 2004 after a long lull in 2003.

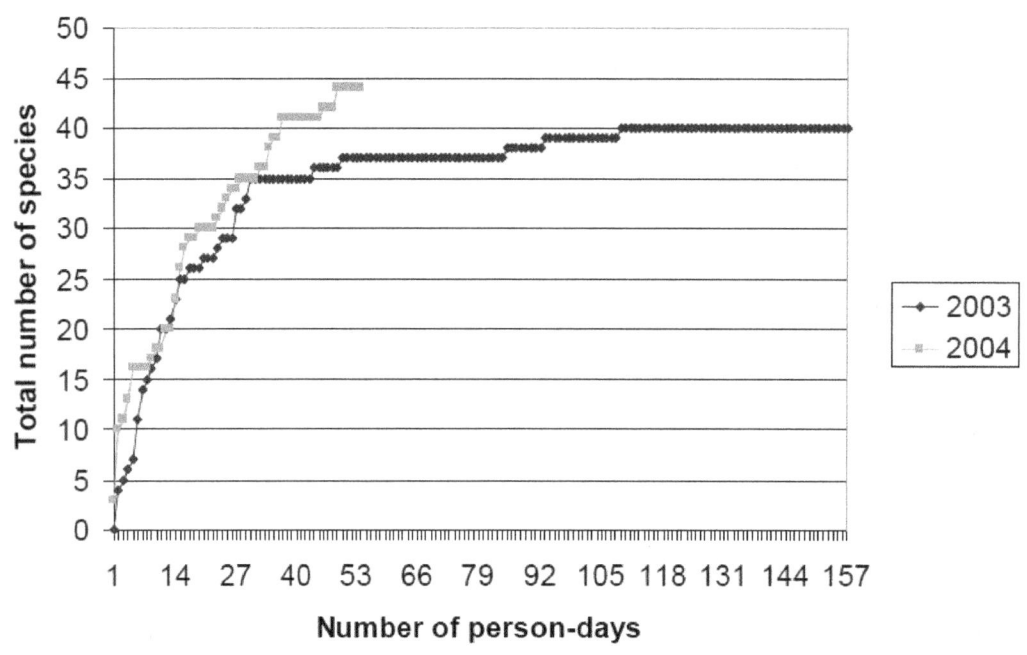

Figure 12. CAVE species curves for 2003 and 2004. This graph illustrates the rate at which we found new species during each year.

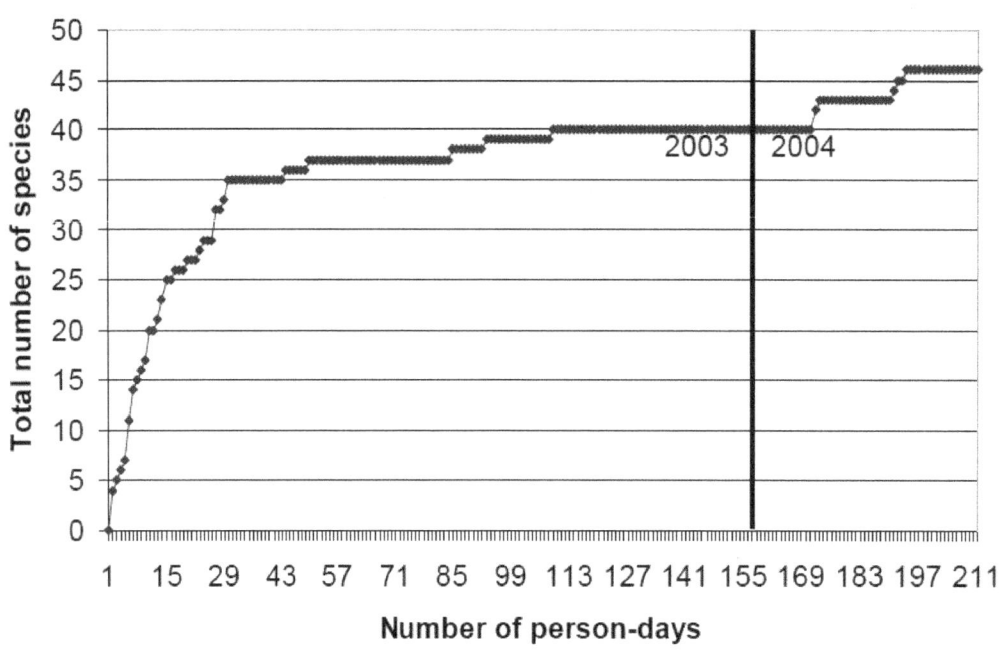

Figure 13. CAVE species curve: 2003-04. This graph illustrates the rate at which we found new species over the two years of the study combined.

Number of Individuals

Table 10 is a list of the number of individuals found of each species, including observations from our crew, Mike Woolman, Chris Newsom, and park staff. This list serves as a rough indication of relative abundance, although it is biased toward conspicuous species and species that live in the areas we searched most often. The table shows that we found six species in 2004 that we did not find in 2003. All the species we found in 2003 we also found in 2004.

We only observed Rio Grande Cooters (*Pseudemys gorzugi*) in Rattlesnake Spring. Because we recounted some of them on separate searches, the listed number of 65 is probably an overestimate of the population. The largest number of turtles we ever saw at one time in the spring was 13.

Comparison of Search Methods

Most of our observations were recorded during foot searches in which we found 2,659 animals (1,706 in 2003; 953 in 2004) comprising 38 species (31 in 2003; 29 in 2004). We incidentally observed 690 animals (400 in 2003; 290 in 2004) comprising 41 species (35 in 2003; 34 in 2004). We captured 117 animals (93 in 2003; 24 in 2004) comprising 16 species (15 in 2003; 8 in 2004) in pitfall traps. We observed 109 animals (85 in 2003; 24 in 2004) comprising 25 species (23 in 2003; 11 in 2004) while road cruising.

Four species were found during foot searches that were not documented using any other search method. These were the Great Plains Toad (*Bufo cognatus*), Western Green Toad (*Bufo debilis insidior*), Yellow Mud Turtle (*Kinosternon flavescens*), and Mexican Spadefoot (*Spea multiplicata*).

Four species were recorded incidentally that were not found by any other method. These were the Ring-necked Snake (*Diadophis punctatus*), Mexican Hog-nosed Snake (*Heterodon nasicus kennerlyi*), Gray-banded Kingsnake (*Lampropeltis alterna*), and Ornate Box Turtle (*Terrapene ornata ornata*).

No species were found in pitfall traps or by road cruising that were not also found via another survey method.

Table 10. Number of individuals found at CAVE by species.

Species	Common Name	Number of Individuals		
		2003	2004	Total
Sceloporus cowlesi	Southwestern Fence Lizard	477	69	546
Aspidoscelis exsanguis	Chihuahuan Spotted Whiptail	333	135	468
Aspidoscelis tesselata	Common Checkered Whiptail	329	134	463
Urosaurus ornatus schmidti	Big Bend Tree Lizard	269	25	294
Scaphiopus couchii	Couch's Spadefoot	11	224	235
Sceloporus poinsettii poinsettii	Northern Crevice Spiny Lizard	192	30	222
Bufo speciosus	Texas Toad	7	205	212
Aspidoscelis inornata heptagramma	Trans-Pecos Striped Whiptail	158	26	184
Cophosaurus texanus scitulus	Chihuahuan Greater Earless Lizard	105	41	146
Bufo debilis insidior	Western Green Toad	0	125	125
Crotaphytus collaris	Eastern Collared Lizard	46	36	82
Pseudemys gorzugi	Rio Grande Cooter	23	42	65
Crotalus lepidus lepidus	Mottled Rock Rattlesnake	37	18	55
Crotalus atrox	Western Diamond-backed Rattlesnake	26	17	43
Bufo punctatus	Red-spotted Toad	6	34	40
Coleonyx brevis	Texas Banded Gecko	30	10	40
Uta stansburiana	Common Side-blotched Lizard	28	7	35
Crotalus molossus molossus	Northern Black-tailed Rattlesnake	25	6	31
Masticophis taeniatus	Striped Whipsnake	23	5	28
Rana berlandieri	Rio Grande Leopard Frog	16	10	26
Spea multiplicata	Mexican Spadefoot	0	22	22
Eumeces obsoletus	Great Plains Skink	16	5	21
Masticophis flagellum testaceus	Western Coachwhip	15	6	21
Aspidoscelis gularis gularis	Texas Spotted Whiptail	19	1	20

Table 11. Number of individuals found at CAVE by species (continued).

Species	Common Name	Number of Individuals		
		2003	2004	Total
Phrynosoma cornutum	Texas Horned Lizard	13	5	**18**
Pituophis catenifer affinis	Sonoran Gophersnake	13	5	**18**
Salvadora grahamiae grahamiae	Mountain Patch-nosed Snake	12	4	**16**
Bogertophis subocularis subocularis	Trans-Pecos Ratsnake	10	3	**13**
Eumeces multivirgatus epipleurotus	Variable Skink	8	3	**11**
Elaphe emoryi	Great Plains Ratsnake	6	4	**10**
Rana catesbeiana	American Bullfrog	5	5	**10**
Tantilla hobartsmithi	Smith's Black-headed Snake	5	3	**8**
Diadophis punctatus	Ring-necked Snake	3	4	**7**
Terrapene ornata ornata	Ornate Box Turtle	3	4	**7**
Phrynosoma modestum	Round-tailed Horned Lizard	4	1	**5**
Rhinocheilus lecontei tessellatus	Texas Long-nosed Snake	2	3	**5**
Leptotyphlops dissectus	New Mexico Threadsnake	2	2	**4**
Hypsiglena torquata janii	Texas Nightsnake	2	1	**3**
Thamnophis cyrtopsis cyrtopsis	Western Black-necked Gartersnake	2	1	**3**
Kinosternon flavescens	Yellow Mud Turtle	0	2	**2**
Thamnophis marcianus marcianus	Marcy's Checkered Gartersnake	0	2	**2**
Bufo cognatus	Great Plains Toad	0	2	**2**
Gyalopion canum	Chihuahuan Hook-nosed Snake	1	1	**2**
Heterodon nasicus kennerlyi	Mexican Hog-nosed Snake	1	1	**2**
Sonora semiannnulata semiannulata	Variable Groundsnake	1	1	**2**
Lampropelits alterna	Gray-banded Kingsnake	0	1	**1**

Undocumented Species

According to a list compiled by Dave Roemer (2002), 49 species have been documented within the park boundary. However, we believe that one of these species, the Big Bend Patch-nosed Snake (*Salvadora hexalepis deserticola*) probably does not occur in the park. Only one record of the snake has been documented in the park (CAVE 2115), that from the park's most highly visited area; the next closest specimen of the species was collected over 160.9 kilometers (100 mi) away (Degenhardt et al. 1996). Most likely, the individual collected from the park had been released by a visitor. Another species, Blanchard's Cricket Frog (*Acris crepitans blanchardi*) is thought to have been extirpated from the park (Roemer 2002).

In 2003, we collectively found two species that had not been documented previously – the Mexican Hog-nosed Snake (*Heterodon nasicus kennerlyi*) and Texas Long-nosed Snake (*Rhinocheilus lecontei tessellatus*). Also, Roemer's list does not include Hernandez's Short-horned Lizard (*Phrynosoma hernandesi hernandesi*), which was apparently observed (though not documented) in the park in 1990 (Roemer 2002), bringing the total number of species to 50.

According to the list, four species occur in the park that we did not find, including one lizard, two snakes, and one turtle. In total, assuming that the park list is correct, we documented 92% of the park's reptiles and amphibians.

The following list contains species that probably occur in the park, but that we did not find this year. Locality data in this list comes from Roemer (2002) and Mike Woolman's report.

Reptiles
Lizards
Phrynosoma hernandesi hernandesi – Hernandez's Short-horned Lizard. Apparently one individual of this species was observed, but not documented in any way, at Putman Cabin in 1990 by D. Carruth. Due to the unique body form of horned lizards, and the improbability that some other horned lizard species would occur at such a high elevation, we believe this sighting is credible. This area appears to be very marginal habitat for the species but probably is better than anywhere else in the park.

Snakes
Lampropeltis getula splendida – Desert Kingsnake. Found at Rattlesnake Springs in 1997. Found outside the park near Rattlesnake Springs by Mike Woolman in 2003.

Nerodia erythrogaster transversa – Blotched Watersnake. Collected at Rattlesnake Springs in the past (UMMZ 121693). This species probably inhabits the marshy Nature Conservancy land adjoining the park, entering the park itself only rarely. It may be more likely to enter the park during wet years when individuals may migrate from the Black River.

Turtles
Trachemys scripta elegans – Red-eared Slider. A dead individual of this species was found at Rattlesnake Springs in 1997. Most likely, this turtle occasionally enters Rattlesnake Spring from the Black River during wet years.

The following species may occur at CAVE, though they have never (or at least have not recently) been documented there. This list is also based on Roemer (2002), although we have eliminated some species from his list because we believe their occurrence in the park is unlikely.

Amphibians
Frogs
Acris crepitans blanchardi – Blanchard's Cricket Frog. This species was formerly found at Rattlesnake Springs but has become extirpated from the park. It may re-enter the park from the Black River during wet years.

Eleutherodactylus augusti latrans – Balcones Barking Frog. This species has been found in Chosa Draw, a couple of miles east of Rattlesnake Springs. Barking frogs often occur in very localized populations and only call vigorously a few nights a year, following rains. This species may occur in the park at Rattlesnake Springs, the low areas on the park's south boundary, or perhaps even in Walnut Canyon.

Spea bombifrons – Plains Spadefoot. Although CAVE seems like fairly marginal habitat for this species, it possibly occurs in the Rattlesnake Springs or other low-lying areas of the park.

Salamanders
Ambystoma tigrinum mavortium – Barred Tiger Salamander. Occasional individuals may enter the park during wet years.

Reptiles
Lizards
Aspidoscelis marmorata – Marbled Whiptail. This species may inhabit the lowest elevation areas of the park.

Gambelia wislizenii – Long-nosed Leopard Lizard. This species may inhabit the lowest elevations of the park near Rattlesnake Springs, the sewage treatment ponds area, or the low area near the mouth of Slaughter Canyon.

Holbrookia maculata – Common Lesser Earless Lizard. This species may inhabit the lowest elevation areas of the park.

Sceloporus magister bimaculosus – Twin-spotted Spiny Lizard. This species may inhabit the lowest elevation areas of the park.

Snakes
Arizona elegans – Glossy Snake. This species may inhabit the lowest elevation areas of the park.

Crotalus viridis viridis – Green Prairie Rattlesnake. This species may inhabit the lowest elevation areas of the park. Rattlesnake Springs is the most likely area.

Lampropeltis triangulum – Milksnake. This species potentially could occur just about anywhere in the park, although it's a long shot.

Leptotyphlops humilis segregus – Trans-Pecos Threadsnake. This species may inhabit the lowest elevation areas of the park.

Tantilla nigriceps – Plains Black-headed Snake. This species may inhabit the lowest elevation areas of the park.

Thamnophis proximus diabolicus – Arid Land Ribbonsnake. This species may enter the park during wet years at either Rattlesnake Springs or in the northwest corner of the park through some of the canyons with pools.

Turtles
Apalone spinifera emoryi – Texas Spiny Softshell. This species may occasionally enter Rattlesnake Springs from the Black River during wet years.

Chelydra serpentina serpentina – Eastern Snapping Turtle. This species may occasionally enter Rattlesnake Springs from the Black River during wet years.

Chrysemys picta bellii – Western Painted Turtle. This species may occasionally enter Rattlesnake Springs from the Black River during wet years.

Figure 14. Mottled Rock Rattlesnake (Crotalus lepidus lepidus) at CAVE. Photo by Mike Woolman.

Fort Davis National Historic Site
Fort Davis National Historic Site, in Jeff Davis County, Texas, covers just 191.8 hectares (474 ac) in the Davis Mountains. This small park, established to protect fort ruins,

includes steep cliffs, rocky hills, flat desert-scrubland, and a cottonwood grove, all within an elevation range of 1,487.4 to 1,591.1 meters (4,880 to 5,220 ft).

At FODA, Sul Ross State University student Adrienne Dreyfus greatly enhanced the effectiveness of our inventory effort by conducting several searches for reptiles and amphibians at the park in 2003 while we were elsewhere. Due to the small size of the park, we were able to survey most of it. There were only a few areas that we did not visit, where large, sheer cliff faces made access impossible. However, we concentrated most of our search effort in Hospital Canyon, the flats surrounding and north of the fort ruins, and the trail system.

Figure 15 shows the locations of all of the reptiles and amphibians we found. Adrienne Dreyfus' data is included in this map. The dots on the map do not indicate our total search area, because we searched some areas without finding any animals, but the map can be used to show roughly where we conducted surveys.

In 2003, we conducted surveys at FODA on May 11-12, June 8-10, July 18-22, August 4-5, and August 18-19. Adrienne Dreyfus visited the park several times during May-August. In 2004, Ian Murray and/or Dave Prival surveyed FODA on June 20-22, July 5-6, July 19-21, August 2-4, August 15-16, August 27-28, and September 14.

Species List
Including the 167 animals recorded by Adrienne Dreyfus, we found 761 reptiles and amphibians in 2003 and 400 in 2004. This totals 1,161 reptiles and amphibians representing 29 species, including five frogs and toads, 12 lizards, 11 snakes, and one turtle (Table 11).

One of the species, the Texas Horned Lizard (*Phrynosoma cornutum*) is state-threatened. We did not find any federally-listed or non-native amphibians or reptiles.

49

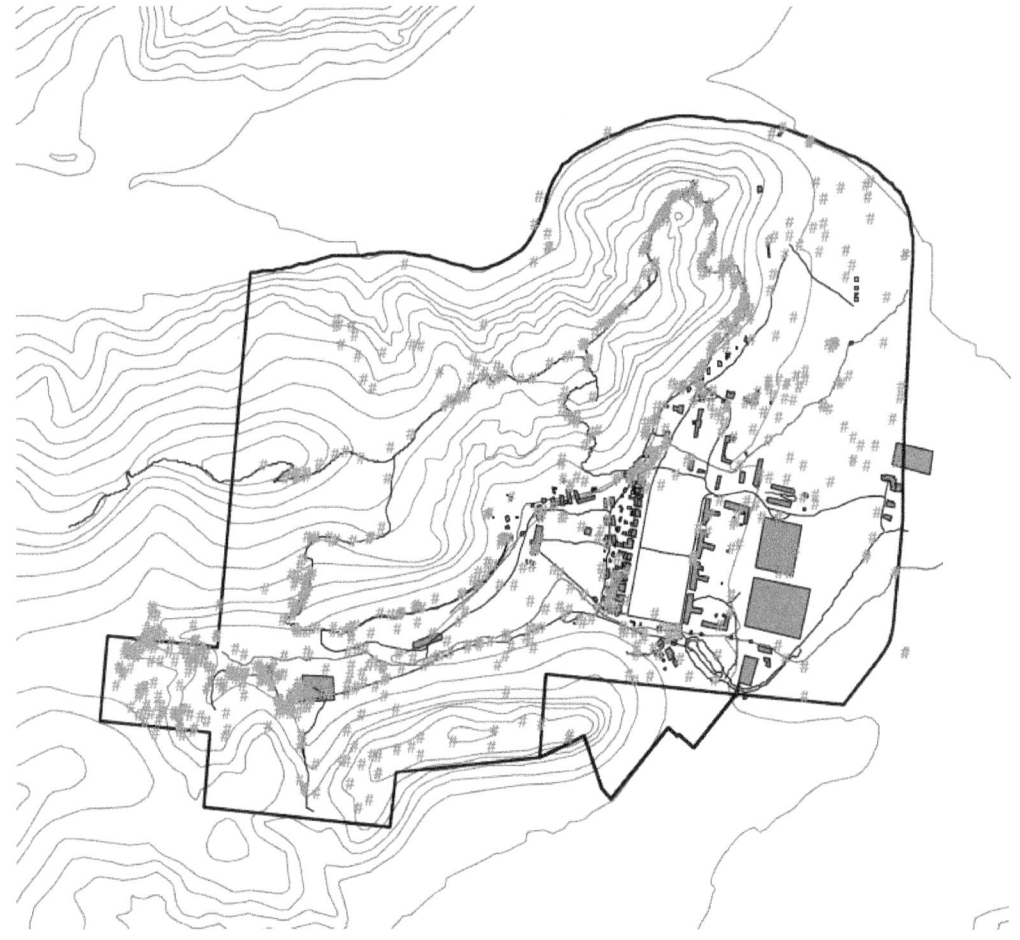

Figure 15. Locations of reptiles and amphibians found at FODA, 2003-04.

Table 11. Species list for Fort Davis National Historic Site.
Scientific names from Conant and Collins (1998) are in parentheses.

AMPHIBIANS
ORDER ANURA – FROGS AND TOADS

Family Bufonidae – True Toads
Bufo punctatus – Red-spotted Toad

Family Hylidae – Treefrogs
Hyla arenicolor – Canyon Treefrog

Family Microhylidae – Narrow-mouthed Toads
Gastrophryne olivacea – Great Plains Narrow-mouthed Toad

Family Pelobatidae – Spadefoot Toads
Scaphiopus couchii – Couch's Spadefoot

Family Ranidae – True Frogs
Rana berlandieri – Rio Grande Leopard Frog

REPTILES
ORDER SQUAMATA – LIZARDS AND SNAKES

Suborder Lacertilia – Lizards

Family Gekkonidae – Geckos
Coleonyx brevis – Texas Banded Gecko

Family Iguanidae – Iguanas and Allies
Cophosaurus texanus scitulus - Chihuahuan Greater Earless Lizard
Crotaphytus collaris – Eastern Collared Lizard (Figure 18)
Holbrookia maculata approximans – Speckled Earless Lizard
Phrynosoma cornutum – Texas Horned Lizard
Sceloporus cowlesi – Southwestern Fence Lizard (*Sceloporus undulatus consobrinus*)
Sceloporus poinsettii poinsettii – Northern Crevice Spiny Lizard
Urosaurus ornatus schmidti – Big Bend Tree Lizard

Family Scincidae – Skinks
Eumeces obsoletus – Great Plains Skink
Eumeces tetragrammus brevilineatus – Short-lined Skink

Family Teiidae – Whiptail Lizards
Aspidoscelis exsanguis – Chihuahuan Spotted Whiptail (*Cnemidophorus exsanguis*)
Aspidoscelis gularis gularis – Texas Spotted Whiptail (*Cnemidophorus gularis gularis*)

Suborder Serpentes – Snakes

Family Colubridae – Colubrid Snakes
Hypsiglena torquata janii – Texas Nightsnake
Masticophis flagellum testaceus – Western Coachwhip
Masticophis taeniatus ornatus – Central Texas Whipsnake (*Masticophis taeniatus girardi*)
Pituophis catenifer affinis – Sonoran Gophersnake (*Pituophis melanoleucus affinis*)
Salvadora grahamiae grahamiae – Mountain Patch-nosed Snake
Sonora semiannnulata semiannulata – Variable Groundsnake
Tantilla hobartsmithi – Smith's Black-headed Snake
Thamnophis cyrtopsis cyrtopsis – Western Black-necked Gartersnake

Family Leptotyphlopidae - Threadsnakes
Leptotyphlops dissectus – New Mexico Threadsnake (*Leptotyphlops dulcis dissectus*)

Family Viperidae – Vipers and Pitvipers
Crotalus lepidus lepidus – Mottled Rock Rattlesnake
Crotalus molossus molossus – Northern Black-tailed Rattlesnake

ORDER TESTUDINES – TURTLES
Family Emydidae – Cooters, Sliders, Box Turtles, and Allies
Terrapene ornata – Ornate Box Turtle

Species Curve

Figure 16 shows the rate at which we found species during each field season (including Adrienne Dreyfus' data). Each season is graphed independently, so species found during 2003 are not taken into account when calculating the number of species found in 2004.

We found 28 species in 51 person-days in 2003, and 23 species in 18 person-days in 2004. Although we found species at a slightly faster rate in 2004 than 2003, the much shorter season resulted in our finding fewer species than in the previous year. In 2003, we seemed to be reaching a plateau toward the end of the season. In 2004, the season ended before we reached a plateau.

Figure 17 shows the rate at which we found new species during our entire survey effort, again including Adrienne Dreyfus' data. We found the first 23 species within 24 days. After that, the rate at which we found new species began to level off. We found new species in 2004 at about the same rate as at the end of 2003.

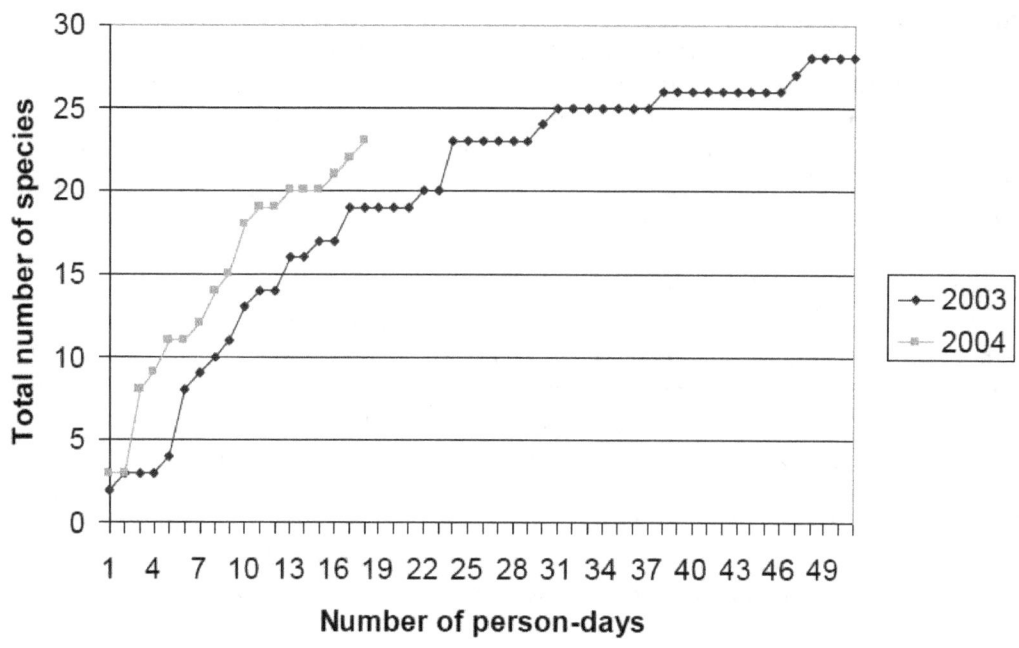

Figure 16. FODA species curves for 2003 and 2004. This graph illustrates the rate at which we found new species during each year.

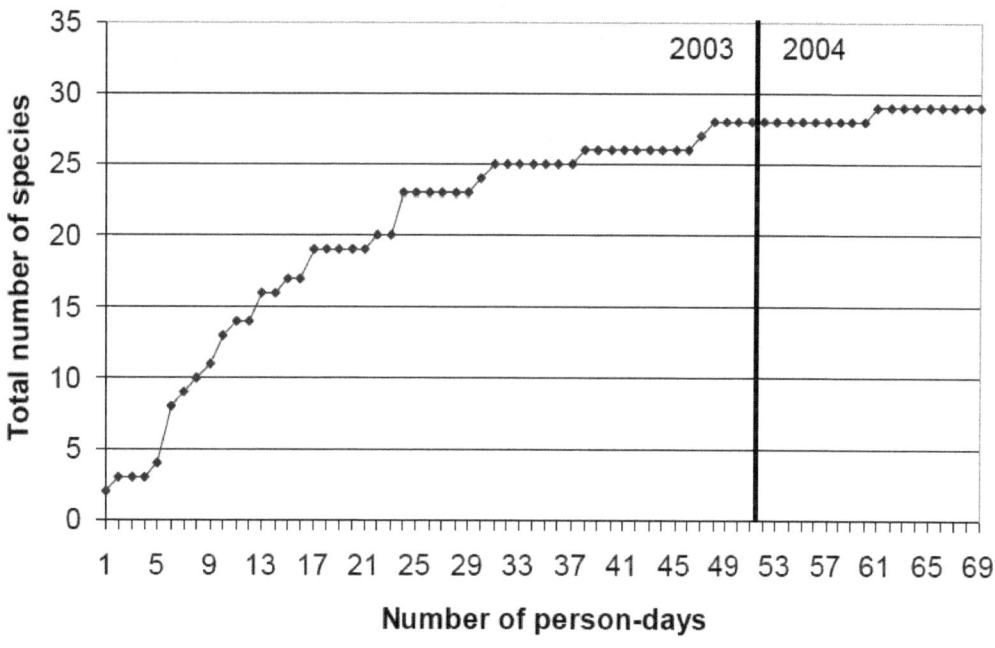

Figure 17. FODA species curve: 2003-04. This graph illustrates the rate at which we found new species over the two years of the study combined.

Number of Individuals

Table 12 is a list of the number of individuals found of each species, including observations from our crew and Adrienne Dreyfus. This list serves as a rough indication of relative abundance, although it is biased toward conspicuous species and species that live in the areas we searched most often. The table shows that we found one species in 2004 that we did not find in 2003. We found six species in 2003 that we did not find in 2004.

Comparison of Search Methods

Most of our observations were recorded during foot searches in which we found 822 animals (632 in 2003; 190 in 2004) comprising 25 species (25 in 2003; 18 in 2004). We incidentally observed 318 animals (112 in 2003; 206 in 2004) comprising 23 species (17 in 2003; 19 in 2004). We captured 21 animals (17 in 2003; 4 in 2004) comprising 9 species (8 in 2003; 2 in 2004) in pitfall traps.

Three species were found during foot searches that were not documented using any other search method. These were the Texas Banded Gecko (*Coleonyx brevis*), Smith's Black-headed Snake (*Tantilla hobartsmithi*), Ornate Box Turtle (*Terrapene ornata*).

Three species were recorded incidentally that were not found by any other method. These were the Eastern Collared Lizard (*Crotaphytus collaris*) (Figure 18), Western Coachwhip (*Masticophis flagellum testaceus*), and Mountain Patch-nosed Snake (*Salvadora grahamiae grahamiae*).

No species were found during formal checks of pitfall traps that were not also found via another survey method. However, the two Great Plains Narrow-mouthed Toads (*Gastrophryne olivacea*) we found were both in pitfall traps, although one was discovered in the pitfall during a foot search.

Table 12. Number of individuals found at FODA by species.

Species	Common Name	Number of Individuals		
		2003	2004	Total
Urosaurus ornatus schmidti	Big Bend Tree Lizard	260	132	**392**
Aspidoscelis exsanguis	Chihuahuan Spotted Whiptail	164	59	**223**
Aspidoscelis gularis gularis	Texas Spotted Whiptail	93	27	**120**
Sceloporus poinsettii poinsettii	Northern Crevice Spiny Lizard	57	54	**111**
Sceloporus cowlesi	Southwestern Fence Lizard	25	51	**76**
Hyla arenicolor	Canyon Treefrog	55	9	**64**
Holbrookia maculata approximans	Speckled Earless Lizard	27	8	**35**
Cophosaurus texanus scitulus	Chihuahuan Greater Earless Lizard	7	19	**26**
Bufo punctatus	Red-spotted Toad	14	4	**18**
Eumeces obsoletus	Great Plains Skink	7	6	**13**
Rana berlandieri	Rio Grande Leopard Frog	6	7	**13**
Eumeces tetragrammus brevilineatus	Short-lined Skink	6	5	**11**
Crotalus lepidus lepidus	Mottled Rock Rattlesnake	5	3	**8**
Hypsiglena torquata janii	Texas Nightsnake	4	4	**8**
Coleonyx brevis	Texas Banded Gecko	5	1	**6**
Crotalus molossus molossus	Northern Black-tailed Rattlesnake	5	1	**6**
Masticophis taeniatus ornatus	Central Texas Whipsnake	3	2	**5**
Scaphiopus couchii	Couch's Spadefoot	4	0	**4**
Gastrophryne olivacea	Great Plains Narrow-mouthed Toad	1	2	**3**
Thamnophis cyrtopsis cyrtopsis	Western Black-necked Gartersnake	1	2	**3**
Leptotyphlops dissectus	New Mexico Threadsnake	2	0	**2**

Table 13. Number of individuals found at FODA by species (continued).

Species	Common Name	Number of Individuals		
		2003	2004	Total
Masticophis flagellum testaceus	Western Coachwhip	2	0	2
Phrynosoma cornutum	Texas Horned Lizard	1	1	2
Pituophis catenifer affinis	Sonoran Gophersnake	1	1	2
Salvadora grahamiae grahamiae	Mountain Patch-nosed Snake	2	0	2
Sonora semiannnulata semiannulata	Variable Groundsnake	2	0	2
Tantilla hobartsmithi	Smith's Black-headed Snake	1	1	2
Crotaphytus collaris	Eastern Collared Lizard (Figure 18)	0	1	1
Terrapene ornata	Ornate Box Turtle	1	0	1

Undocumented Species

Determining the number of species inhabiting FODA is extremely difficult. FODA is a very small park (191.82 hectares [474 ac]), so it probably is a permanent home to few species. However, it is also part of the extremely diverse Davis Mountains, so many species probably move through the park.

The following list contains species that may occur in the park at least occasionally, but that we did not find. In all likelihood, some of these species inhabit the park permanently, some visit the park only rarely, and some are never in the park. However, it is difficult to differentiate between groups without long-term surveys. This list is comprised from range maps and our conjecture regarding whether the species is likely to occur in the habitat types available in the park.

The list of undocumented species includes four frogs and toads, one salamander, five lizards, eleven snakes, and one turtle. If all of these species really occur at FODA, then there are a total of 51 species in the park, of which we documented 57%. Again, our estimate of 51 species should be viewed as highly suspect. The shape of the species curve suggests that we were in fact much closer to our 90% documentation target than our undocumented species list indicates.

Amphibians
Frogs and Toads
Bufo cognatus – Great Plains Toad. Possible in the flats.
Bufo woodhousii australis – Southwestern Woodhouse's Toad. Possible in the flats.
Spea bombifrons – Plains Spadefoot. Possible in the flats.
Spea multiplicata – Mexican Spadefoot. Possible in the flats.

Salamanders

Ambystoma tigrinum mavortium – Barred Tiger Salamander. Possible in the rocky part of Hospital Canyon or on the north side of the park near the creek that runs along the highway.

Reptiles

Lizards

Aspidoscelis inornata heptagramma – Trans-Pecos Striped Whiptail. Possible in the flats.
Aspidoscelis tesselata – Common Checkered Whiptail. Possible in the rocky areas.
Phrynosoma hernandesi hernandesi – Hernandez's Short-horned Lizard. Possible on the ridgetops.
Phrynosoma modestum – Round-tailed Horned Lizard. Possible in the flats.
Sceloporus olivaceus – Texas Spiny Lizard. Collected from area in 1987 (SRSU 5871). Most likely to be found on the large trees in the picnic area.

Snakes

Agkistrodon contortrix pictigaster – Trans-Pecos Copperhead. Possible in Hospital Canyon.
Bogertophis subocularis subocularis – Trans-Pecos Ratsnake. Collected from area in 1968 (Yale 2709). Possible throughout the park.
Crotalus atrox – Western Diamond-backed Rattlesnake. Most likely in the flats.
Diadophis punctatus – Ring-necked Snake. Possible in the flats.
Elaphe bairdi – Baird's Ratsnake. Collected from area in 1968 (Yale 2711). Most likely in rocky areas.
Elaphe emoryi – Great Plains Ratsnake. Collected from area in 1968 (Yale 2719). Possible throughout the park.
Lampropelits alterna – Gray-banded Kingsnake. Most likely in rocky areas.
Lampropeltis triangulum – Milksnake. Possible throughout the park.
Tantilla cucullata – Trans-Pecos Black-headed Snake. Most likely in the flats.
Tantilla nigriceps – Plains Black-headed Snake. Most likely in the flats.
Thamnophis marcianus marcianus - Marcy's Checkered Gartersnake. Collected from area in 1968 (Yale 2737). Most likely in the rocky part of Hospital Canyon or on the north side of the park near the stream along the highway.

Turtles

Kinosternon flavescens – Yellow Mud Turtle. Collected from FODA in 1968 (MSB 20524). Most likely in the rocky part of Hospital Canyon or on the north side of the park near the stream along the highway.

Figure 18. Eastern Collared Lizard (*Crotaphytus collaris*) at FODA. Photo by Ian Murray.

Guadalupe Mountains National Park

Guadalupe Mountains National Park covers 34,971.31 hectares (86,416 ac) of Culberson and Hudspeth Counties, Texas. The park includes the highest point in Texas at 2,666.7 meters (8,749 ft), mid-elevation hills, one of the most well developed riparian areas in the region, and low desert and sand dunes around the park's lowest point at 1,104.6 meters (3,624 ft).

Our searches focused primarily on McKittrick Canyon and the Western Expansion Area. Grace (1980) found high reptile and amphibian diversity in McKittrick Canyon during his surveys, and we intensely surveyed this area hoping to maximize the number of reptile and amphibian species we would find in the park. We intensely searched the Western Expansion Area to find new species characteristic of habitat found only in this section of the park (e.g., creosote flats, gypsum dunes), and also to document species composition and distribution in this previously unsurveyed part of the park. Other areas we searched included those in and near The Bowl, Dog Canyon, Patterson Hills, Williams Ranch House, Choza Springs, Smith and Manzanita Springs, Pine Springs, and Salt Basin.

Figure 19 shows the locations of all of the reptiles and amphibians we found. The dots on the map do not indicate our total search area, because we searched several areas without finding any animals, but the map can be used to show roughly where we conducted surveys.

In 2003, we conducted surveys at GUMO on May 9-10, June 11-22, July 10-18, August 20-26, and August 29 for a total of 79 person-days. In 2004, Allison Ebner was stationed at GUMO from June 14 to August 3, and Ian Murray was stationed at GUMO from August 20 to August 30. In addition, Dave Prival made several trips to the park and boot camp training was held there. In total, we surveyed GUMO for 74 person-days in 2004.

A weak monsoon season and overall dry conditions likely hurt our search efforts at GUMO in 2003, as we never experienced precipitation heavy enough or long enough to induce seasonal amphibians to call and aggregate at seasonal ponds. Although we don't have weather data specific to GUMO, nearby Carlsbad, NM, had precipitation levels that were 75% below normal from June to September according to National Weather Service Data.

The following year was much wetter, but this did not seem to greatly influence herp activity in the park. Most park staff reported seeing fewer snakes in 2004 than in previous years, and we never heard any amphibians other than Rio Grande leopard frogs (*Rana berlandieri*) calling from within the park.

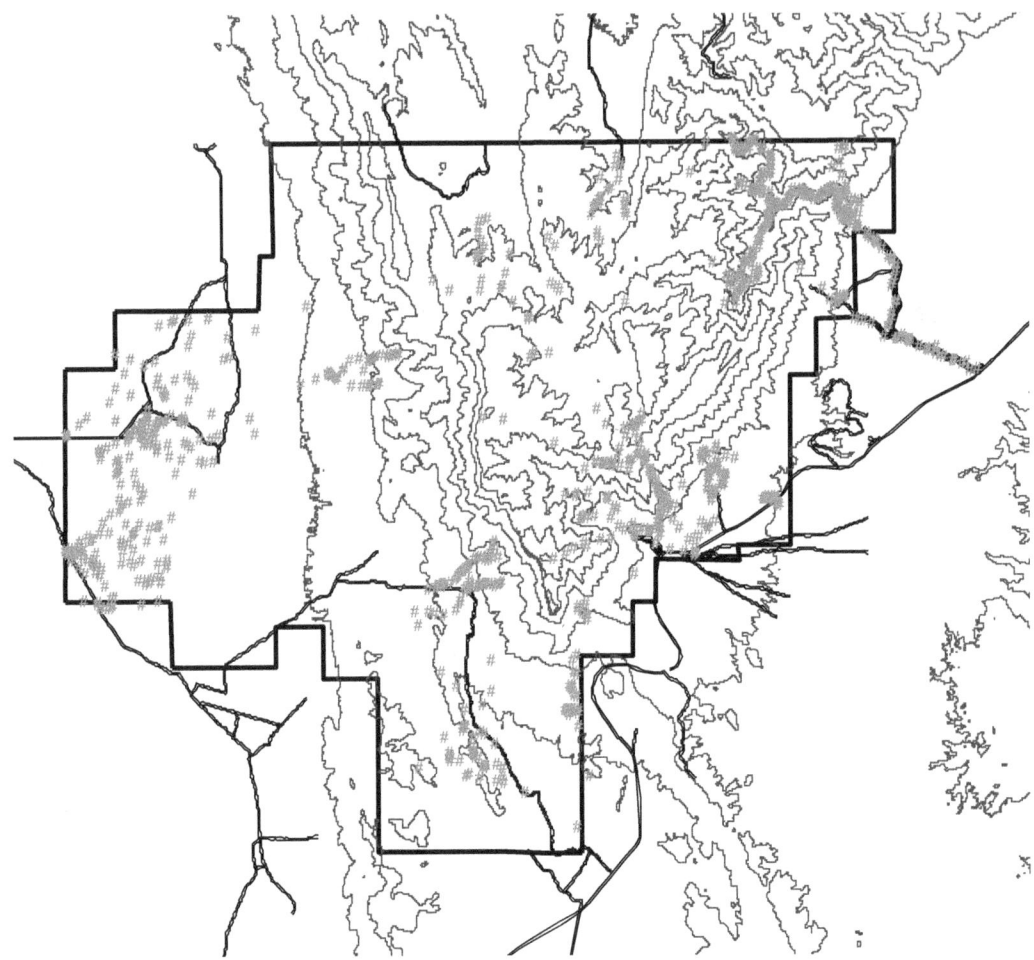

Figure 19. Locations of reptiles and amphibians found at GUMO, 2003-04.

Species List

Including the 57 animals recorded by park staff, we found 1,073 reptiles and amphibians at GUMO in 2003 and 858 in 2004. This totals 1,931 reptiles and amphibians at GUMO representing 48 species, including seven frogs and toads, 18 lizards, 21 snakes, and two turtles (Table 13).

The Texas Horned Lizard (*Phrynosoma cornutum*) and Hernandez's Short-horned Lizard (*Phrynosoma hernandesi hernandesi*) are classified as Threatened by the Texas Parks and Wildlife Department. We did not find any federally-listed amphibians and reptiles or non-native species.

We found nine species that were previously undocumented in the park. Eight of these species were thought likely to occur there based on similar habitat and nearby localities following Grace (1980) and Werler and Dixon (2000), or they had been previously observed by Grace in the Western Expansion Area, which was not part of the park when he did his survey in the late 1970s. We found seven of these previously undocumented species in the Western Expansion Area. They are the Great Plains Toad (*Bufo cognatus*), Plains Spadefoot (*Spea bombifrons*) (Figure 22), Common Lesser Earless Lizard (*Holbrookia maculata*), Chihuahuan Hook-nosed Snake (*Gyalopion canum*), Texas Nightsnake (*Hypsiglena torquata janii*), Texas Long-nosed Snake (*Rhinocheilus lecontei tessellatus*), and Mexican Hog-nosed Snake (*Heterodon nasicus kennerlyi*). The eighth new species, the Trans-Pecos Ratsnake (*Bogertophis subocularis subocularis*) was found in the Patterson Hills.

In addtion to the eight species listed above, we found one species, the Trans-Pecos Threadsnake (*Leptotyphlops humilis segregus*), that appears to be a significant range extension. We found two of these snakes in the Western Expansion Area.

Table 13. Species list for Guadalupe Mountains National Park.
Scientific names from Conant and Collins (1998) are in parentheses.

AMPHIBIANS
ORDER ANURA – FROGS AND TOADS

Family Bufonidae – True Toads
Bufo cognatus - Great Plains Toad
Bufo punctatus – Red-spotted Toad
Bufo speciosus – Texas Toad

Family Pelobatidae – Spadefoot Toads
Scaphiopus couchii – Couch's Spadefoot
Spea bombifrons – Plains Spadefoot (Figure 22)
Spea multiplicata – Mexican Spadefoot

Family Ranidae – True Frogs
Rana berlandieri – Rio Grande Leopard Frog

REPTILES
ORDER SQUAMATA – LIZARDS AND SNAKES

Suborder Lacertilia – Lizards

Family Gekkonidae – Geckos
Coleonyx brevis – Texas Banded Gecko

Family Iguanidae – Iguanas and Allies
Cophosaurus texanus scitulus – Chihuahuan Greater Earless Lizard
Crotaphytus collaris – Eastern Collared Lizard
Gambelia wislizenii – Long-nosed Leopard Lizard
Holbrookia maculata – Common Lesser Earless Lizard
Phrynosoma cornutum – Texas Horned Lizard
Phrynosoma hernandesi hernandesi – Hernandez's Short-horned Lizard (*Phyrnosoma douglasii hernandesi*)
Phrynosoma modestum – Round-tailed Horned Lizard

Sceloporus cowlesi – Southwestern Fence Lizard (*Sceloporus undulatus consobrinus*)
Sceloporus poinsettii poinsettii – Northern Crevice Spiny Lizard
Urosaurus ornatus schmidti – Big Bend Tree Lizard
Uta stansburiana – Common Side-blotched Lizard

Family Scincidae – Skinks
Eumeces multivirgatus epipleurotus – Variable Skink
Eumeces obsoletus – Great Plains Skink

Family Teiidae – Whiptail Lizards
Aspidoscelis exsanguis – Chihuahuan Spotted Whiptail (*Cnemidophorus exsanguis*)
Aspidoscelis inornata heptagramma – Trans-Pecos Striped Whiptail (*Cnemidophorus inornatus heptagrammus*)
Aspidoscelis marmorata marmorata – Western Marbled Whiptail (*Cnemidophorus marmoratus*)
Aspidoscelis tesselata – Common Checkered Whiptail (*Cnemidophorus tesselatus*)

Suborder Serpentes – Snakes

Family Colubridae – Colubrid Snakes
Arizona elegans elegans – Kansas Glossy Snake
Bogertophis subocularis subocularis – Trans-Pecos Ratsnake
Diadophis punctatus – Ring-necked Snake
Elaphe emoryi – Great Plains Ratsnake (*Elaphe guttata emoryi*)
Gyalopion canum – Chihuahuan Hook-nosed Snake
Heterodon nasicus kennerlyi – Mexican Hog-nosed Snake
Hypsiglena torquata janii – Texas Nightsnake
Masticophis flagellum testaceus – Western Coachwhip
Masticophis taeniatus – Striped Whipsnake
Pituophis catenifer affinis – Sonoran Gophersnake (*Pituophis melanoleucus*)
Rhinocheilus lecontei tessellatus – Texas Long-nosed Snake
Salvadora grahamiae grahamiae – Mountain Patch-nosed Snake
Sonora semiannulata semiannulata – Variable Groundsnake
Tantilla hobartsmithi – Smith's Black-headed Snake
Thamnophis cyrtopsis cyrtopsis – Western Black-necked Gartersnake

Family Leptotyphlopidae – Blindsnakes
Leptotyphlops dissectus – New Mexico Threadsnake (*Leptotyphlops dulcis dissectus*)
Leptotyphlops humilis segregus – Trans-Pecos Threadsnake

Family Viperidae – Vipers and Pitvipers
Crotalus atrox – Western Diamond-backed Rattlesnake
Crotalus lepidus lepidus – Mottled Rock Rattlesnake
Crotalus molossus molossus – Northern Black-tailed Rattlesnake
Crotalus viridis viridis – Green Prairie Rattlesnake

ORDER TESTUDINES – TURTLES

Family Kinosternidae – Mud Turtles
Kinosternon flavescens – Yellow Mud Turtle

Family Emydidae – Cooters, Sliders, Box Turtles, and Allies
Terrapene ornata luteola – Desert Box Turtle

Species Curve

Figure 20 shows the rate at which we found species during each field season (not including park staff observations). Each season is graphed independently, so species found during 2003 are not taken into account when calculating the number of species found in 2004.

In 2003, the rate at which we found new species began to level off after 38 person-days, within which we found 38 species. In 2004, the curve levels off after 32 person-days with just 29 species, although we had another spurt of new species at the end of the 2004 field season.

Figure 21 shows the rate at which we found new species during our entire survey effort (not including park staff observations). The rate at which we found new species leveled off after 65 person-days with 44 species documented. We found only four additional species during 2004, mostly right at the end of the field season.

Number of Individuals

Table 14 is a list of the number of individuals we found of each species, including both our data and data collected by park staff. This list serves as a rough indication of relative abundance, although it is biased toward conspicuous species and species that live in the areas we searched most often. The table shows that we found three species in 2004 that we did not find in 2003. We found ten species in 2003 that we did not find in 2004.

Comparison of Search Methods

Most of our observations were recorded during foot searches in which we found 1,580 animals (968 in 2003; 612 in 2004) comprising 46 species (43 in 2003; 31 in 2004). We incidentally observed 249 animals (72 in 2003; 177 in 2004) comprising 26 species (16 in 2003; 22 in 2004). We observed 38 animals (8 in 2003; 30 in 2004) comprising six species (2 in 2003; 6 in 2004) while road cruising. Finally, we found 64 animals (25 in 2003; 39 in 2004) consisting of 11 species (6 in 2003; 8 in 2004) in pitfall traps.

We found 14 species during foot searches that we did not document using any other method. These species were the Great Plains Toad (*Bufo cognatus*), Trans-Pecos Ratsnake (*Bogertophis subocularis subocularis*), Texas Banded Gecko (*Coleonyx brevis*), Eastern Collared Lizard (*Crotaphytus collaris*), Mottled Rock Rattlesnake (*Crotalus lepidus lepidus*), Green Prairie Rattlesnake (*Crotalus viridis viridis*), Great Plains Ratsnake (*Elaphe emoryi*), Variable Skink (*Eumeces multivirgatus epipleurotus*),

Chihuahuan Hook-nosed Snake (*Gyalopion canum*), Mexican Hog-nosed Snake (*Heterodon nasicus kennerlyi*), Common Lesser Earless Lizard (*Holbrookia maculata*), Trans-Pecos Threadsnake (*Leptotyphlops humilis segregus*), Texas Long-nosed Snake (*Rhinocheilus lecontei tessellatus*), and Plains Spadefoot (*Spea bombifrons*) (Figure 22).

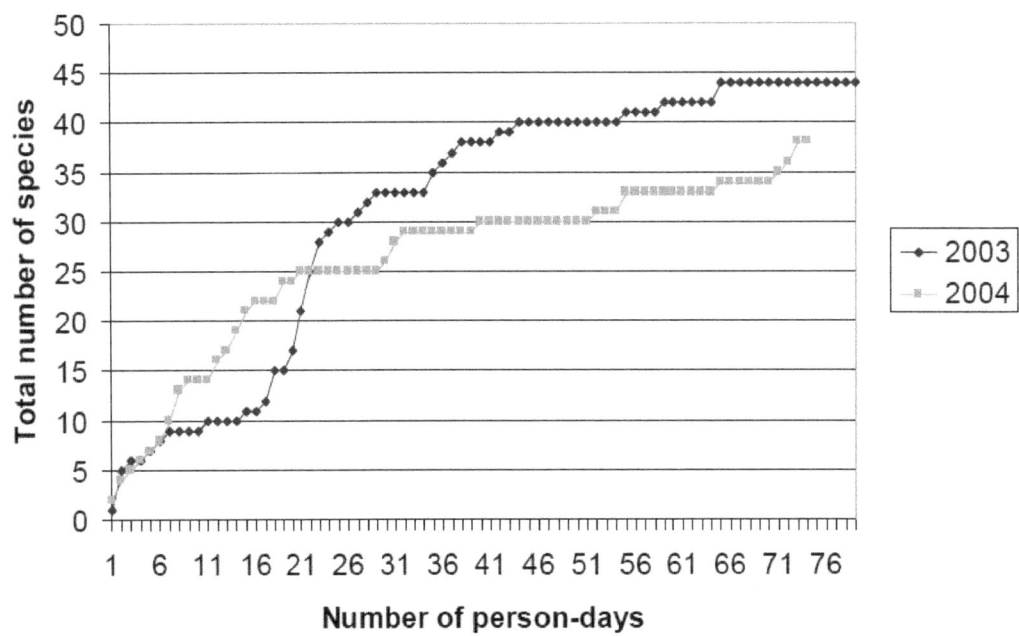

Figure 20. GUMO species curves for 2003 and 2004. This graph illustrates the rate at which we found new species during each year.

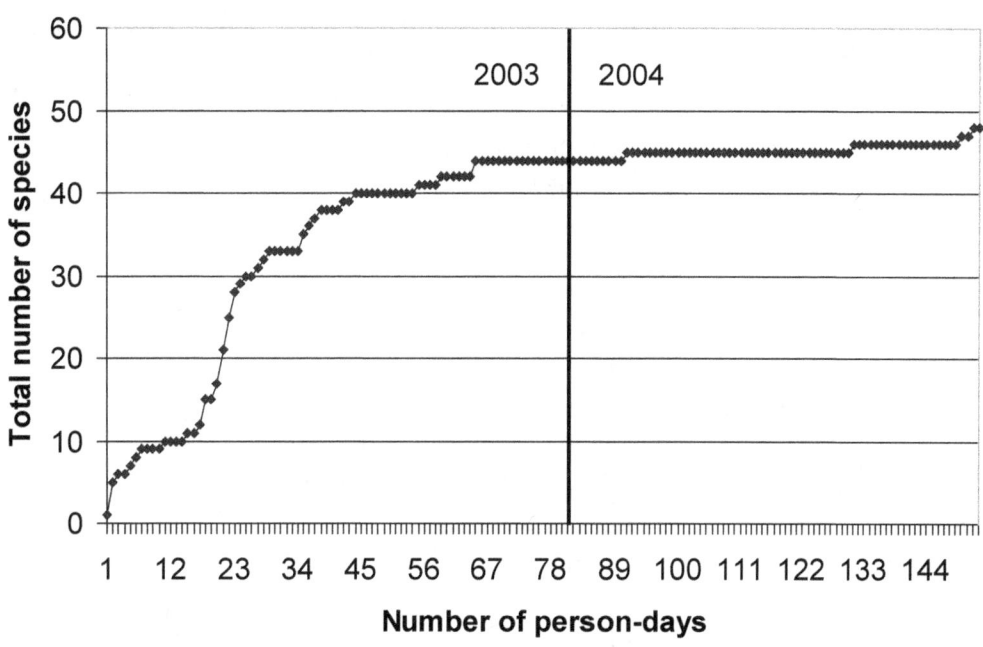

Figure 21. GUMO species curve: 2003-04. This graph illustrates the rate at which we found new species over the two years of the study combined.

Table 14. Number of individuals found at GUMO by species.

Species	Common Name	Number of Individuals		
		2003	2004	Total
Rana berlandieri	Rio Grande Leopard Frog	291	61	**352**
Aspidoscelis exsanguis	Chihuahuan Spotted Whiptail	114	213	**327**
Sceloporus cowlesi	Southwestern Fence Lizard	154	150	**304**
Urosaurus ornatus schmidti	Big Bend Tree Lizard	128	92	**220**
Sceloporus poinsettii poinsettii	Northern Crevice Spiny Lizard	107	35	**142**
Cophosaurus texanus scitulus	Chihuahuan Greater Earless Lizard	63	48	**111**
Aspidoscelis marmorata marmorata	Western Marbled Whiptail	21	65	**86**
Uta stansburiana	Common Side-blotched Lizard	29	51	**80**
Bufo punctatus	Red-spotted Toad	10	28	**38**
Aspidoscelis inornata heptagramma	Trans-Pecos Striped Whiptail	11	17	**28**
Eumeces obsoletus	Great Plains Skink	16	8	**24**
Aspidoscelis tesselata	Common Checkered Whiptail	9	12	**21**
Gambelia wislizenii	Long-nosed Leopard Lizard	7	9	**16**
Crotalus atrox	Western Diamond-backed Rattlesnake	7	8	**15**
Spea bombifrons	Plains Spadefoot (Figure 22)	15	0	**15**
Terrapene ornata luteola	Desert Box Turtle	6	9	**15**
Scaphiopus couchii	Couch's Spadefoot	4	9	**13**
Coleonyx brevis	Texas Banded Gecko	3	8	**11**
Phrynosoma cornutum	Texas Horned Lizard	8	3	**11**
Crotalus molossus molossus	Northern Black-tailed Rattlesnake	6	2	**8**
Phrynosoma modestum	Round-tailed Horned Lizard	5	3	**8**

Table 15. Number of individuals found at GUMO by species (continued).

Species	Common Name	Number of Individuals		
		2003	**2004**	**Total**
Phrynosoma hernandesi hernandesi	Hernandez's Short-horned Lizard	5	2	7
Diadophis punctatus	Ring-necked Snake	6	0	6
Masticophis taeniatus	Striped Whipsnake	3	3	6
Sonora semiannulata semiannulata	Variable Groundsnake	5	1	6
Thamnophis cyrtopsis cyrtopsis	Western Black-necked Gartersnake	5	1	6
Bufo speciosus	Texas Toad	0	5	5
Gyalopion canum	Chihuahuan Hook-nosed Snake	3	2	5
Leptotyphlops dissectus	New Mexico Threadsnake	2	3	5
Crotalus viridis viridis	Green Prairie Rattlesnake	2	2	4
Hypsiglena torquata janii	Texas Nightsnake	1	3	4
Salvadora grahamiae grahamiae	Mountain Patch-nosed Snake	3	1	4
Spea multiplicata	Mexican Spadefoot	2	2	4
Crotalus lepidus lepidus	Mottled Rock Rattlesnake	3	0	3
Crotaphytus collaris	Eastern Collared Lizard	3	0	3
Eumeces multivirgatus epipleurotus	Variable Skink	0	3	3
Kinosternon flavescens	Yellow Mud Turtle	3	0	3
Pituophis catenifer	Gophersnake	1	2	3
Tantilla hobartsmithi	Smith's Black-headed Snake	2	1	3
Arizona elegans elegans	Kansas Glossy Snake	1	1	2
Bufo cognatus	Great Plains Toad	2	0	2
Bogertophis subocularis subocularis	Trans-Pecos Ratsnake	0	2	2
Heterodon nasicus kennerlyi	Mexican Hog-nosed Snake	1	1	2
Leptotyphlops humilis segregus	Trans-Pecos Threadsnake	1	1	2
Rhinocheilus lecontei tessellatus	Texas Long-nosed Snake	2	0	2
Elaphe emoryi	Great Plains Ratsnake	1	0	1
Holbrookia maculata	Common Lesser Earless Lizard	1	0	1
Masticophis flagellum testaceus	Western Coachwhip	1	0	1

The only species we observed incidentally and did not document by another method was a Western Coachwhip (*Masticophis flagellum testaceus*).

We did not capture any species in pitfall traps that we did not also find using another method.

We found one species, the Texas Toad (*Bufo speciosus*), by road cruising and no other method.

Undocumented Species

Following a list compiled by Grace (1980) and locality data found in Werler and Dixon (2000), there are probably seven species of reptiles and amphibians in GUMO that we have yet to find, including one toad, one salamander, one lizard, and four snakes. If this estimate is correct, there are 55 species of reptiles and amphibians in GUMO, and we found 87% of them.

We believe that the following species are likely to occur at GUMO although we did not find them during our inventory. This list is based on Grace (1980) and Werler and Dixon (2000).

Amphibians
Frogs and Toads
Bufo debilis insidior – Western Green Toad. Grace (1980) cites one locality from Parker's Tank 2.4 km (1.5 mi) east of Ship on the Desert and one from Ship on the Desert.

Salamanders
Ambystoma tigrinum mavortium – Barred Tiger Salamander. Grace (1980) cites personal observations of this species in earthen tanks in The Bowl as recently as 1979 (although these tanks have apparently not held water since then), and one record from 3.2 km (2 mi). southwest of Pine Springs on Highway 62/180 (also from 1979).

Reptiles
Lizards
Sceloporus magister bimaculosus – Twin-spotted Spiny Lizard. Grace (1980) cites one Sul Ross State University voucher record taken from near Able and Eclipse Wells in the Western Expansion Area.

Snakes
Crotalus scutulatus – Mohave Rattlesnake. Grace (1980) cites two records for this species. One specimen is from the gypsum sand dunes west of Eclipse Well in what is now the Western Expansion Area. The other specimen comes from Highway 62/180 18 km (11.2 mi) southwest of Pine Springs. We observed this species outside the park west of the Western Expansion Area in 2004.

Lampropeltis alterna – Gray-banded Kingsnake. Grace (1980) cites one record from the park from the southeast side of Hunter Peak. This species likely inhabits this habitat and lower elevations elsewhere in the park but remains undetected due to its rarity and secretive nature.

Lampropeltis getula splendida – Desert Kingsnake. Grace (1980) cites two specimens from Highway 62/180 that are 11 and 16 km (6.8 and 9.9 mi) southwest of Pine Springs Headquarters and outside the park's boundaries. This species most likely occurs in the lower elevations typical of the southern and western areas of the park.

Tantilla nigriceps – Plains Black-headed Snake. Grace (1980) collected one specimen from outside the park 9.7 km (6 mi). southwest of Pine Springs on Highway 62/180. He suggested the species very likely occurs at lower elevations in the park.

The following species may occur at GUMO, though they have never been documented here. This list is based on Grace (1980), Werler and Dixon (2000), and Degenhardt et al. (1996).

Amphibians
Frogs and Toads
Eleutherodactylus augusti latrans – Balcones Barking Frog. This species has been heard calling near Rattlesnake Springs in Carlsbad Caverns National Park and could exist in GUMO. This species often calls only a few nights a year, often centered around the first heavy summer rainfall. Consequently it is not easily detected and could exist in rodent burrows in the west side of the park or in limestone cliffs and fissures in higher elevations in the park.

Rana catesbeiana – American Bullfrog. This species probably does not occur in the park, as their loud, distinct calls would likely reveal their presence. However, given that McKittrick Canyon, Smith Spring, and Manzanita Spring all receive considerable visitor pressure, it is possible they could be introduced by the public and ultimately invade freshwater areas in the park. This is something that the park should do everything within its power to avoid.

Lizards
Aspidoscelis gularis gularis – Texas Spotted Whiptail. This species occurs nearby at Carlsbad Caverns National Park and could occupy GUMO on flat ground at low elevations.

Snakes
Opheodrys vernalis – Smooth Greensnake. Grace (1980) cites two records for this species based on sight observations of other people, and one record of vertebral remains in Upper Sloth Cave. Werler and Dixon (2000) show no voucher records of this species in Texas within at least 321.87 kilometers (200 mi). Degenhardt et al. (1996) show one specimen more than 80.5 kilometers (50 mi) away in New Mexico. This species is extremely unlikely in the park, but if it does exist, it would be found at mid to high elevations. Mostly likely it has been extirpated from the park.

Sistrurus catenatus edwardsii – Desert Massassauga. This species has been vouchered over 80.5 kilometers (50 mi) away in southern New Mexico (Degenhardt et al. 1996) and prefers desert grasslands and shortgrass prairies. If it occurs in GUMO, it would likely be found in the grassy, low elevation areas near Dog Canyon. There are also reports of this species in the Salt Basin area (J. Mueller, pers. com.).

Thamnophis marcianus marcianus – Marcy's Checkered Gartersnake. Grace (1980) did not believe this species occurred in the park, but the GUMO amphibian and reptile checklist, which was updated by Brent Wauer in 1991, cites one record from McKittrick Canyon Road (Grace and Wauer 1991). We do not know if this record represents a voucher specimen, or merely an observation.

Trimorphodon biscutatus vilkinsonii – Texas Lyresnake. Grace (1980) cites vertebral remains of this species from Upper Sloth Cave in the park. The next closest known locality for this species is in the Franklin Mountains near El Paso (Werler and Dixon 1996). This species is especially secretive and might inhabit the rockier and more arid parts of the park.

Figure 22. Plains Spadefoot (*Spea bombifrons*) at GUMO. Photo by Dan Moen.

White Sands National Monument

White Sands National Monument covers 58,166.68 hectares (143,733 ac) in Otero and Doña Ana Counties, New Mexico. It protects about 50% of the world's largest gypsum sand dune field. Although most of the park consists of sand dune, there is a strip of desert scrub and a large playa on the west side.

At WHSA, our efforts were supplemented in 2003 by the work of Biological Technician Mike Swink, who ran pitfall traps with the assistance of Park Biologist Bill Conrod and other staff. Mike constructed two additional pitfall trap arrays (with the help of Bill' Conrod) . Mike also occasionally recorded incidental observations of reptiles and amphibians.

During 2004, Chris Teske surveyed the park, as a part-time job, during the first half of the field season; he subsequently had to work full-time at another job. Dave Furphy surveyed the park during the second half of the season; unfortunately some of the data he collected is missing, possibly because there was a long delay between collecting the data and downloading it into a computer.

One of the major obstacles we faced at WHSA was access to the west side of the park, which contains most of the park's non-sand dune habitat and is therefore likely to be home to many species not found elsewhere. In order to reach the west side, one must drive across the White Sands Missile Range. We had to obtain permission to cross the range several days in advance, use a park vehicle, and be accompanied at all times by our park contact, Bill Conrod. During our last visits in 2003, we were finally able to obtain our own security badges in order to visit the area independently, but for most of the 2003 season and all of the 2004 season we could only survey the area if accompanied by park staff. Due to the long, irregular search periods required for herp survey work, these requirements severely hampered our efforts in this part of the park.

Although we do not have weather data, the monsoon rains apparently missed WHSA in 2003. However, there was a significant rain event on the west side of the park in August 2004 that brought several breeding toad choruses into action in and around Lake Lucero.

Figure 23 shows the locations of all of the reptiles and amphibians we found. Mike Swink's data is included in this map. The dots on the map do not indicate our total search area, because we searched some areas without finding any animals, but the map can be used to show roughly where we conducted surveys.

In 2003, we conducted surveys at WHSA on May 6, June 30-July 3, July 28-29, and September 2-3 for a total of 27 person-days. Mike Swink worked at the park from late May to mid-September.

In 2004 we ended up with only 15 person-days at the park due in part to the loss of our first field technician part way through the field season, followed by the loss of some data from our second field technician.

Figure 23. Locations of reptiles and amphibians found at WHSA, 2003-04.

Species List

Including the 237 animals recorded by Mike Swink and park staff, we found 476 reptiles and amphibians in 2003 and 334 in 2004. This totals 810 reptiles and amphibians at WHSA representing 28 species, including six toads, 10 lizards, 11 snakes, and one turtle (Table 15).

We did not find any state-listed, federally-listed, or non-native amphibians or reptiles.

Table 15. Species list for White Sands National Monument.
Scientific names from Stebbins (2003) are in parentheses.

AMPHIBIANS
ORDER ANURA – FROGS AND TOADS

Family Bufonidae – True Toads
Bufo cognatus – Great Plains Toad

Table 16. Species list for White Sands National Monument (continued).

Bufo debilis insidior – Western Green Toad
Bufo punctatus – Red-spotted Toad

Family Pelobatidae – Spadefoot Toads
Scaphiopus couchii – Couch's Spadefoot
Spea bombifrons – Plains Spadefoot
Spea multiplicata – Mexican Spadefoot

REPTILES
ORDER SQUAMATA – LIZARDS AND SNAKES

Suborder Lacertilia – Lizards

Family Iguanidae – Iguanas and Allies
Crotaphytus collaris – Eastern Collared Lizard
Gambelia wislizenii – Long-nosed Leopard Lizard
Holbrookia maculata ruthveni – Bleached Earless Lizard
Phrynosoma modestum – Round-tailed Horned Lizard
Sceloporus cowlesi – Southwestern Fence Lizard (*Sceloporus undulatus consobrinus/cowlesi*)
Sceloporus magister bimaculosus – Twin-spotted Spiny Lizard
Uta stansburiana – Common Side-blotched Lizard

Family Teiidae – Whiptail Lizards
Aspidoscelis gypsi – Little White Whiptail (*Cnemidophorus inornatus*)
Aspidoscelis inornata llanuras – Plains Striped Whiptail (*Cnemidophorus inornatus*)
Aspidoscelis marmorata marmorata – Western Marbled Whiptail (*Cnemidophorus tigris marmoratus*)

Suborder Serpentes – Snakes

Family Colubridae – Colubrid Snakes
Arizona elegans philipi – Painted Desert Glossy Snake (Figure 26)
Hypsiglena torquata janii – Texas Nightsnake
Lampropeltis getula splendida – Desert Kingsnake
Masticophis flagellum testaceus – Western Coachwhip
Pituophis catenifer affinis – Sonoran Gophersnake
Rhinocheilus lecontei tessellatus – Texas Long-nosed Snake
Tantilla nigriceps – Plains Black-headed Snake

Family Leptotyphlopidae - Threadsnakes
Leptotyphlops humilis segregus – Trans-Pecos Threadsnake

Family Viperidae – Vipers and Pitvipers
Crotalus atrox – Western Diamond-backed Rattlesnake
Crotalus viridis viridis – Green Prairie Rattlesnake
Sistrurus catenatus edwardsii – Desert Massasauga (skeleton only)

Table 16. Species list for White Sands National Monument (continued).

ORDER TESTUDINES – TURTLES

Family Emydidae – Cooters, Sliders, Box Turtles, and Allies
Terrapene ornata luteola – Desert Box Turtle

Species Curve
Figure 24 shows the rate at which we found species during each field season (not including data collected by park staff). Each season is graphed independently, so species found during 2003 are not taken into account when calculating the number of species found in 2004.

We did not seem to reach a real plateau in either year. Each year we found new species throughout the field season.

Figure 25 shows the rate at which we found new species during our entire survey effort (again not including park staff data). This figure is affected by lost data since we don't know how many person-days were lost during 2004, although we do know that no new species were found during those days. We continued to find new species throughout the survey period. It is possible that we finally reached a plateau after 40 person-days when we had documented 28 species, but is also possible that we would continue to find new species with additional search effort.

Number of Individuals
Table 16 is a list of the number of individuals we found of each species, including observations from our crew and park staff. This list serves as a rough indication of relative abundance, although it is biased toward conspicuous species and species that live in the areas we searched most often. All the species we found in 2004 had been found in 2003. However, we found ten species in 2003 that we did not find in 2004.

Comparison of Search Methods
Most of our observations were recorded during foot searches in which we found 360 animals (265 in 2003; 95 in 2004) comprising 22 species (17 in 2003; 11 in 2004). We incidentally observed 230 animals (95 in 2003; 135 in 2004) comprising 21 species (20 in 2003; 10 in 2004). We captured 219 animals (116 in 2003; 103 in 2004) comprising 16 species (14 in 2003; 9 in 2004) in pitfall and funnel traps. Finally, we did not find any animals by road cruising in 2003, but did find one animal while road cruising in 2004.

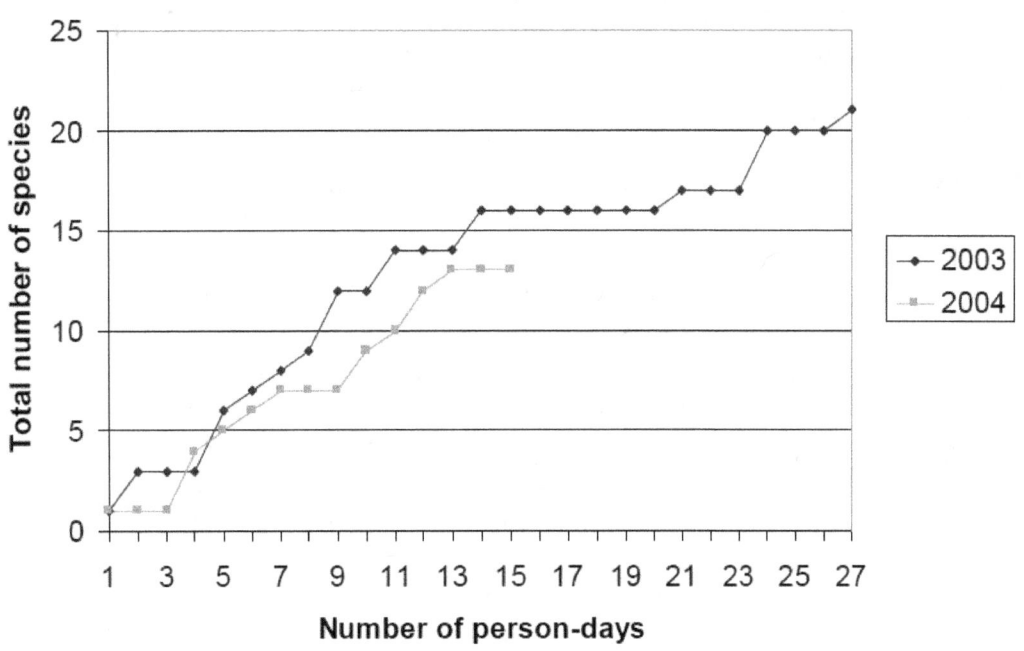

Figure 24. WHSA species curves for 2003 and 2004. This graph illustrates the rate at which we found new species each year.

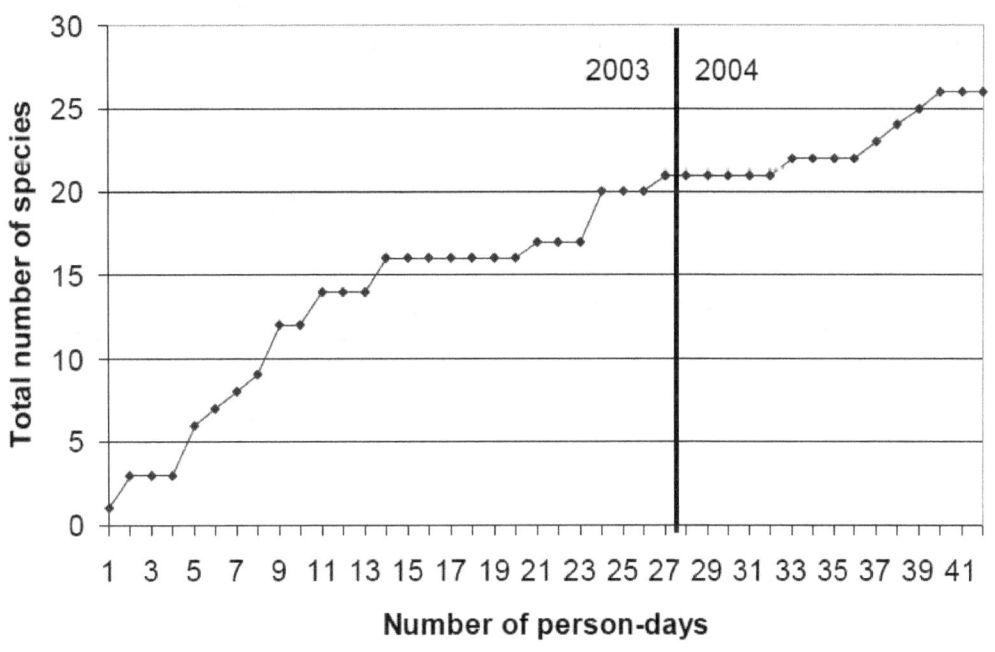

Figure 25. WHSA species curve: 2003-04. This graph illustrates the rate at which we found new species over the two years of the study combined.

Table 16. Number of individuals found at WHSA by species.

Species	Common Name	Number of Individuals		
		2003	2004	Total
Uta stansburiana	Common Side-blotched Lizard	155	85	**240**
Aspidoscelis marmorata marmorata	Western Marbled Whiptail	73	50	**123**
Bufo debilis insidior	Western Green Toad	17	58	**75**
Aspidoscelis gypsi	Little White Whiptail	61	3	**64**
Bufo punctatus	Red-spotted Toad	1	60	**61**
Sceloporus cowlesi	Southwestern Fence Lizard	43	13	**56**
Aspidoscelis inornata llanuras	Plains Striped Whiptail	37	15	**52**
Holbrookia maculata ruthveni	Bleached Earless Lizard	28	0	**28**
Spea bombifrons	Plains Spadefoot	2	18	**20**
Sceloporus magister bimaculosus	Twin-spotted Spiny Lizard	12	6	**18**
Scaphiopus couchii	Couch's Spadefoot	4	12	**16**
Spea multiplicata	Mexican Spadefoot	1	5	**6**
Crotalus viridis viridis	Green Prairie Rattlesnake	5	0	**5**
Gambelia wislizenii	Long-nosed Leopard Lizard	3	2	**5**
Masticophis flagellum testaceus	Western Coachwhip	5	0	**5**
Tantilla nigriceps	Plains Black-headed Snake	4	1	**5**
Arizona elegans philipi	Painted Desert Glossy Snake (Figure 26)	3	1	**4**
Crotaphytus collaris	Eastern Collared Lizard	4	0	**4**
Hypsiglena torquata janii	Texas Nightsnake	4	0	**4**
Leptotyphlops humilis segregus	Trans-Pecos Threadsnake	4	0	**4**
Crotalus atrox	Western Diamond-backed Rattlesnake	1	2	**3**
Rhinocheilus lecontei tessellatus	Texas Long-nosed Snake	2	1	**3**
Bufo cognatus	Great Plains Toad	1	1	**2**
Phrynosoma modestum	Round-tailed Horned Lizard	1	1	**2**
Pituophis catenifer affinis	Sonoran Gophersnake	2	0	**2**
Lampropeltis getula splendida	Desert Kingsnake	1	0	**1**
Sistrurus catenatus edwardsii	Desert Massasauga	1	0	**1**
Terrapene ornata luteola	Desert Box Turtle	1	0	**1**

During foot searches, only one species was found that was not documented using any other search method - the Desert Massasauga (*Sistrurus catenatus edwardsii*).

One species was recorded incidentally that was not found by any other method - the Desert Box Turtle (*Terrapene ornata luteola*).

One species was found in a pitfall/funnel trap that was not recorded by any other method – the Desert Kingsnake (*Lampropeltis getula splendida*).

Undocumented Species

Prior to our survey, Jerry Johnson and Doug Burkett, two herpetologists with extensive experience in the WHSA area, provided written comments on the existing WHSA list of reptiles and amphibians, giving us a good baseline of potentially occurring species to work from. The following list, including the locality information, is based mostly on their comments. We have excluded a few species from their list because we do not believe suitable habitat exists in the park.

The list of undocumented species that are likely to occur in the park includes one salamander, four lizards, and five snakes. If this list is accurate, there are 38 species inhabiting the park, of which we collectively documented 74%.

Amphibians
Salamanders
Ambystoma tigrinum mavortium – Barred Tiger Salamander. Found on the road to Garton Pond in 1976. Most likely to be found near Garton Pond during a very wet year.

Reptiles
Lizards
Aspidoscelis exsanguis – Chihuahuan Spotted Whiptail. Has been found near the park. Most likely to be found on the west side.
Aspidoscelis neomexicana – New Mexico Whiptail. Probably inhabits desert flats and arroyos on the west side of the park.
Cophosaurus texanus scitulus – Chihuahuan Greater Earless Lizard. Has been found outside WHSA just west of the park. Most likely to be found on the west side.
Phrynosoma cornutum – Texas Horned Lizard. Has been found outside the park. Most likely to be found on the west side.

Snakes
Heterodon nasicus – Western Hog-nosed Snake. Was collected from the park in 1977 and observed near the housing area in 1983. Most likely to be found in grassy areas near the dunes.
Masticophis taeniatus taeniatus – Desert Striped Whipsnake. Has been found west of the park. Most likely to be found on the west side.
Salvadora hexalepis deserticola – Big Bend Patch-nosed Snake. Has been found just west of the park. Most likely to be found on the west side.
Sonora semiannulata semiannulata – Variable Groundsnake. Has been found near the park. Most likely to be found on the west side.
Thamnophis cyrtopsis cyrtopsis – Western Black-necked Gartersnake. Has been found west of the park. Most likely to be found on the west side.

Johnson and Burkett also list the following species as potentially occurring in the park, but questionable.

Reptiles

Lizards

Eumeces obsoletus – Great Plains Skink. Has been found outside WHSA in the arroyos west of the park. Most likely to be found on the west side.

Urosaurus ornatus schmidti – Big Bend Tree Lizard. May not occur in the park, but has been found in low numbers in arroyos west of the park. Most likely to be found on the west side.

Snakes

Diadophis punctatus – Ring-necked Snake. May occur in the creosote flats or the west side.

Gyalopion canum – Chihuahuan Hook-nosed Snake. Unlikely to occur in the park, but possible. Most likely to be found on the west side or south of the highway.

Salvadora grahamiae grahamiae – Mountain Patch-nosed Snake. Usually found at higher elevations, but have been found down low on the Missile Range. Most likely to be found on the west side.

Tantilla hobartsmithi – Smith's Black-headed Snake. Unlikely, but has been found in the lower Sacramento Mountains near Alamogordo. Most likely to be found on the west side.

Figure 26. Painted Desert Glossy Snake (Arizona elegans philipi) at WHSA. Photo by James Borgmeyer.

Discussion

One of the stated goals of the inventory was to document 90% of the reptile and amphibian species at each park. We believe that we surpassed 90% at CAVE (92%), and came very close at GUMO (87%) and BIBE (86%). We were a bit farther from our goal at AMIS (82%) and WHSA (74%), and may not have been close to 90% at FODA (57%).

However, we may have been closer to 90% at AMIS and FODA than our estimates indicate because it is difficult to be certain which species are present in those parks. Although AMIS is a large park, it is extremely narrow and almost all of it consists of heavily disturbed areas which may not be attractive to some of the local herpetofauna. It is even more difficult to know which species are likely to occur at FODA due to its extremely small size. The strong plateaus apparent at the end of both the AMIS and FODA species curves suggest that we were, in fact, quite close to documenting 90% of the species in each of these parks.

Our relatively low number of documented species at WHSA is due in part to the logistical difficulties that limited our search time in the park. However, given that almost all of the "undocumented" species likely to occur at WHSA are most likely to occur on the west side of the park only, we believe that the primary problem was the regulatory restrictions imposed by the White Sands Missile Range that kept us from spending much time in that part of the park.

The most important function of an inventory is that it provides a snapshot of the species present in an area at a given point in time. However, this information will lose its value over time unless repeat surveys are conducted to examine how the reptile and amphibian community changes or remains stable.

This report and appendices include several types of data that can be used to establish monitoring programs to detect changes within the herpetofaunal community that may occur as a result of climate change, urbanization on the park boundary, drought, non-native species invasion, wildland fire, or other factors. However, different monitoring strategies come with different pros and cons. We can evaluate some of these strategies by viewing each year of our study as a separate inventory.

Strategy 1: Monitoring Species Composition

The species list itself serves as a baseline for what species were present in 2003-04. However, due to the secretive nature of many reptiles and amphibians, as well as their sporadic activity patterns, monitoring species composition may not be a simple task. This approach would only work if you could count on finding the same species each time. However, during both 2003 and 2004, we found species that we did not find in the other year in five out of the six parks (Table 17).

Table 17. Apparent changes in species composition during study.
This table lists the number of species found in each year that were not found in the other year of the survey. It also lists the number of species found in both years (i.e., the more "reliable" species), what percentage these reliable species comprise of the total species found, and the apparent percent change in species composition between the two years.

	Number of species found in 2003 only	Number of species found in 2004 only	Number of species found in both years	% of reliable species out of total species found	Apparent % change in species composition
AMIS	7	9	29	64.4%	35.6%
BIBE	3	15	41	69.5%	30.5%
CAVE	0	6	40	87.0%	13.0%
FODA	6	1	22	75.9%	24.1%
GUMO	10	3	35	72.9%	27.1%
WHSA	10	0	18	64.3%	35.7%

We do not believe it is likely that any species were permanently extirpated from any of the parks between 2003 and 2004, or that new species colonized any of the parks during our study. Therefore, Table 17 indicates that if an intensive inventory is conducted in a park in a given year, the data can indicate that 13 to 36% of the species have either colonized or been extirpated from the park since the previous inventory even if there is no actual change in species composition.

Although it is true that search effort was not equal during both years of our study, we found a greater number of unique species in the year with less search effort in 33% of the parks, indicating that search effort alone cannot account for these annual differences.

Weather conditions are clearly a major factor in the success of a herpetological inventory in a given year. For example, we found six species at CAVE in 2004 that we did not find in 2003, but did not find any species in 2003 that we did not also find in 2004. Most likely, this is partly because 2003 was a dry year, whereas 2004 was wet. However, at GUMO, located just south of CAVE, we had the opposite trend – in 2003 we found ten species that we did not find in 2004, but only found three species in 2004 that were not found the previous year.

Therefore, simply comparing wet years to wet years and dry years to dry years is not likely to make comparing annual species lists a more reliable monitoring method. The skill of the researchers involved, natural population level fluctuations, pure luck, and other factors that may be difficult to identify and impossible to account for are likely to always skew species lists from year to year. As such, a simple comparison of species lists over the years is unlikely to reliably indicate whether the herpetological community is changing or remaining stable.

Another option is to just monitor the reliable species – those that can always be documented in an inventory. This means conceding that the rare species (the species most likely to be extirpated) cannot be monitored. There are two important things to keep in mind if this option is selected. First, the reliable species make up a smaller percentage of the total than it seems. For example, at GUMO, 72.9% of the species we found were documented in both years (hence, reliable), but we did not document 100% of the species. If our estimate that we documented 87% of the species in the park is correct, then just 63.4% of the park's species could be considered reliable. Therefore, over one third of the park's herp species could theoretically be wiped out before the species being monitored are affected (assuming that the rare species are likely to be extirpated before the common species).

Second, the number of reliable species will decrease with every inventory until a plateau is reached, even if the species composition does not change. This is because many of the reliable species from our study are based on observations of just one or a few individuals each year. It doesn't require much bad luck to miss one individual in a given inventory, so these relatively rare reliable species will prove unreliable as inventories continue, until only the most common species remain.

Using GUMO as an example again, let us assume that over time, species will only be reliably documented if we found more than five individuals during each of our two survey years. Those species for which we found five individuals or less in a season are likely to be overlooked during some later inventory just by chance. This reduces the number of reliable species from 35 to 15, so now we are just monitoring 27% of the species likely to occur in the park. A series of repeated inventories could probably succeed in determining whether these 15 species remain present in the park or not. However, we are monitoring the 15 species that are probably the least likely to be extirpated. Table 18 indicates how many species could be monitored in each park using these same criteria.

Table 18. Long-term reliable species.
Long-term reliable species are defined as those species for which we found >5 individuals during each year. Because we are uncertain of the total number of species present in some parks, we calculate these long-term reliables as a percentage both of the number of species we actually found and the number of species we listed as likely to occur.

	Number of long-term reliable species	Percent of total species found	Percent of total species likely to occur
AMIS	16	35.6%	29.1%
BIBE	20	33.9%	29.0%
CAVE	19	41.3%	38.0%
FODA	10	34.5%	19.6%
GUMO	15	31.2%	27.3%
WHSA	6	21.4%	15.8%

Strategy 2: Monitoring Species Richness

Another strategy is to monitor species richness, the number of species present. By monitoring the number of species found during a survey period, rather than the species themselves, one rare species can essentially substitute for another rare species, which should reduce the natural variation between surveys. We can use our data to compare how apparent species richness changed between years in our survey (Table 19).

It is unlikely that there was any real, long-term change in species richness in any of the parks during our two year study. Therefore, the apparent percent change in Table 19 illustrates the error that would result if one attempted to monitor species richness using these two years of data. As predicted, monitoring species richness seems to be more reliable than monitoring species composition. On average, species composition changed by 27.7% between years, whereas species richness changed by 19.5%. Nonetheless, clearly there can be dramatic apparent annual fluctuations in species richness even if there is no actual change.

Of course, there should be less error in estimating variation in either species composition or species richness if several years of data are pooled and then compared with other data sets that also consist of several years of pooled data. However, as Tables 18 and 20 demonstrate, there can be very large apparent annual fluctuations so many years of data would have to be pooled in order to reduce the error to an acceptable level.

Table 19. Apparent changes in species richness during study
This table lists the total number of species found each year, as well as the apparent percent change in species richness between 2003 and 2004.

	Total number of species found in 2003	Total number of species found in 2004	Apparent % change in species richness between 2003 and 2004
AMIS	36	38	+ 5.6%
BIBE	44	56	+ 27.3%
CAVE	40	46	+ 15.0%
FODA	28	23	- 17.9%
GUMO	45	38	- 15.6%
WHSA	28	18	- 35.7%

Strategy 3: Monitoring Species Distribution

A third monitoring strategy is to use the maps we created of the locations of individuals of each species to monitor distribution. One would expect that prior to extirpation there should be a detectable change in the distribution of a given species. For example, if the range of a species that was widespread in 2003 becomes very limited by 2013, we would suspect that this species is in some trouble. Monitoring distribution could be particularly effective for documenting the effects of climate change on herpetofauna, because we can predict that most species are likely to move to higher elevations as the climate warms.

As such, species that are typically found only within a certain elevational range in a park are likely to be the best candidates for using distribution monitoring to detect changes in the herpetofauna community.

An advantage to monitoring species distribution instead of species composition or species richness is that changes in distribution may give advance warning that a species is in trouble, whereas the other methods just tell you when a species that was formerly present becomes absent, by which time it may be too late to implement any conservation measures for that species.

However, species distribution does have the same disadvantage as the other monitoring methods – it will probably only be possible to monitor changes in distribution of common or highly visible species. If rare species are not found in an area where they used to be found or suddenly appear in a new area, it is likely that they were just overlooked in some of the inventories.

An additional disadvantage of monitoring species distribution is that there may be natural fluctuations as populations have good years and bad years, so it is possible that a range extension or contraction may just be a normal event and not a cause for concern. However, since long-term herpetological studies are rare, and very little information is available regarding small-scale changes in distribution over time of various species, several years of monitoring will be required before any natural fluctuation patterns can be identified.

Strategy 4: Monitoring Relative Abundance

Another tool that can be used for monitoring is relative abundance. We recorded every reptile and amphibian we saw in each park during 2003-04. We can use these data to calculate which species are common relative to other species. Although these data are biased toward areas we searched, we covered enough of each park that any major shifts in relative abundance should be apparent through monitoring. It will be important to standardize the survey design for monitoring if relative abundance is monitored. The data also are biased toward conspicuous species, although that bias should be the same in all surveys, so this should not be a problem for monitoring.

As with the other monitoring strategies, monitoring relative abundance is likely to be possible only with common species. One way to monitor relative abundance is to rank species in terms of abundance and compare ranks. Table 20 lists the number of species with the same rank in each year among the top 10 most abundant species each year, the number of species that were among the top five species in both years, and the number of species that were among the top 10 in both years.

Table 20. Similarities in relative abundance between 2003 and 2004.
Species were ranked in terms of relative abundance for each year. The first column shows how many species had the same rank both years, only considering the 10 most abundant species for each year (maximum value possible = 10). The second column shows how many species were among the top five most abundant in both years (maximum value possible = 5), and the third column shows how many were among the top 10 in both years (maximum value possible = 10).

Park	Number of species with same rank both years		Number of species in top 5 both years		Number of species in top 10 both years	
	All herps	Reptiles only	All herps	Reptiles only	All herps	Reptiles only
AMIS	2	2	3	4	9	9
BIBE	1	1	3	4	8	8
CAVE	0	0	2	3	5	9
FODA	2	3	4	4	9	9
GUMO	2	0	4	3	8	9
WHSA	1	3	2	4	6	7

Unlike the other parameters considered for monitoring, relative abundance actually did change at some parks between 2003 and 2004. The most apparent difference was in amphibian populations, which may be dramatically larger or smaller from one year to the next depending upon precipitation. However, because we are more interested in monitoring long-term trends than natural annual fluctuations, we will need to find a way of using relative abundance in such a way that these fluctuations do not affect the data if we are going to monitor relative abundance.

Table 20 indicates that a simple comparison of rank is not going to be very useful for monitoring, because few species retain the same rank in consecutive years. However, it may be more useful to look at whether common species remain common. So, we could look at how many of the five most common species are the same each year, or how many of the ten most common species are the same each year.

Table 20 indicates that while the top five most common species may change from year to year, the top ten are relatively stable. At every park except CAVE and WHSA, eight or nine species remained in the top ten each year. One reason this number is not higher is that amphibian populations fluctuate so dramatically. So, if we just look at reptiles instead, we can achieve a more stable top ten list. Nine of the species are in the top ten both years in four of the six parks, and eight are in the top ten in both years in one other. At WHSA, only seven reptile species were in the top ten both years, but this may be a function of the relatively small sample size at WHSA. Also, the number of species within the top ten at all parks should be much more consistent if the same areas are monitored each time.

A disadvantage of monitoring relative abundance in this way is that once again, we are only monitoring the most common species (in this case, the ten most common). However, an advantage of monitoring relative abundance over monitoring species composition or species richness is that you may be able to detect trends while there is still time to do something about it. For example, if a species that has been consistently among the ten most common drops off the top ten list for a few years, it will tell you that this species may be becoming more rare and should be investigated. In contrast, by the time the species drops entirely off the species list, it may be too late for conservation measures.

Implementing a Monitoring Program

As the above section on monitoring strategies indicates, we have to recognize that we will not be able to monitor rare species, at least not at a park-wide level. Instead, we are only likely to be able to detect changes in common and/or conspicuous species. Obviously, this is not ideal, because in most cases we would expect the rare species to be at a greater extirpation risk than the common species.

Of the four monitoring strategies outlined, we recommend creating a monitoring program that will emphasize the ability to detect changes in distribution and relative abundance rather than species composition or species richness, because distribution and relative abundance are more likely to provide information on important community-level changes in time to take conservation measures. Species composition and richness should be recorded also; however, these parameters are less likely to indicate that something bad is happening until it is too late.

In order to monitor any of these aspects – species composition, species richness, distribution, or relative abundance – additional surveys will need to be carried out. When designing monitoring surveys for reptiles and amphibians, assuming that funds and manpower are in short supply (as expected), one faces two options.

The first option is to set up monitoring plots or transects that can be repeated every year, several times a year. In theory this could be accomplished by as few as one or two people working one or two days a week during the active season, depending on the size of the areas to be monitored.

Although randomly placed plots or transects would allow the greatest level of inference to the rest of the park, a completely randomized approach will probably not be feasible with the limited resources likely to be available, because reptiles and amphibians are not randomly distributed. In order to have any power to detect change, plots and transects will have to be placed in areas of high reptile and amphibian abundance and/ or diversity.. Plots or transects may be able to be randomly placed within these areas for slightly greater inferential power.

Because randomization will not be feasible in most parks, it will not be possible to use plots or transects to monitor herpetofauna on a park-wide or region-wide basis using this approach. However, it should be possible to detect significant changes in species richness, distribution, or relative abundance within areas that are particularly favorable to reptiles and amphibians. Changes observed in these areas may serve as a warning that something may be occurring park-wide.

In addition, the distribution of common species within the park can be monitored relatively easily if long transects (i.e., several kilometers in length) are occasionally surveyed each year. Most parks have a trail system that could be used as an easily repeatable transect. Although, again, the results will only apply to the area surveyed, because the transects will not be located randomly, changes observed could serve as a warning that something is happening park-wide that warrants closer investigation. For parks with significant elevational gradients (such as BIBE and GUMO), distribution transects should include all elevations.

The second option is to save the money that would have been spent on a limited annual monitoring effort and instead conduct a complete herpetological inventory every five to ten years. Any inventory should run for at least two summers in order to reduce the chance that an abnormally dry or wet year will greatly influence the results. If conducted in approximately the same way each time, using approximately the same methods, one should be able to compare distribution and relative abundance between inventories, and species composition and richness by comparing pooled inventories.

The advantage to this approach is that large parts of each park can be surveyed, so you will have a much better idea of which species, if any, have changed distributions. The large number of individuals and species recorded during an inventory also makes statistical comparisons of species richness and relative abundance more robust than may be possible with annual monitoring.

The main disadvantage is that a lot can happen in ten years, and it may take several inventories to identify any major trends, by which time it will likely to be too late to do anything. Also, if one inventory occurs during two wet years and another during two dry years, it may be difficult to draw conclusions from the results.

Our analysis of monitoring strategies provides some insights regarding how well conducting repeat, large-scale inventories could work as a monitoring method. In order to determine whether repeat, small-scale monitoring could be worthwhile, we set up a monitoring route in every park except WHSA during 2004. We provide the results in detail below to give park managers an idea of what they can expect to achieve with low-cost surveys.

At AMIS, the same route in Evans Canyon was surveyed on four mornings. The first and third surveys were conducted under relatively similar weather conditions (Surveys 1 and 3 [respectively]: start temperature = 28.3° C, 28.1° C; RH = 80%, 86%; Cloud cover = 0%, 90%; end temperature = 34.6°C, 34.8°C; RH = 51%, 52%; Cloud cover = 0%, 20%). The second and fourth surveys were also conducted under relatively similar weather conditions (Surveys 2 and 4 [respectively]: start temperature = 23.1°C, 22.9°C; RH = 72%, 100%; Cloud cover = 75%, 95%; end temperature = 25.8°C, 25.1°C, RH = 60%, 91%; Cloud cover = 70%, 95%).

Ten species were found during these surveys, although only four were observed on every survey (*Aspidoscelis gularis gularis* [Texas Spotted Whiptail], *Sceloporus merriami merriami* [Merriam's Canyon Lizard], *Sceloporus poinsettii poinsettii* [Northern Crevice

Spiny Lizard], and *Urosaurus ornatus schmidti* [Big Bend Tree Lizard]). Six species were found on both Surveys 1 and 3, and four species were observed on both Surveys 2 and 4. Species richness on the four surveys was 6, 6, 9, and 4, respectively. *Sceloporus merriami merriami* (Merriam's Canyon Lizard) and *Sceloporus poinsettii poinsettii* (Northern Crevice Spiny Lizard) were always the two most common species.

At BIBE, we set up a driving monitoring transect along the road between Castolon and the Santa Elena Canyon parking area. Because of frequent road closures due to flooding throughout the summer of 2004, we could only run this transect three times. All transects were driven at night. Weather conditions were relatively similar during each transect (start temperature range = 32.4 to 32.7°C, RH range = 25 to 39%, cloud cover range = 0 to 80%; end temperature range = 32.1 to 33.7°C, RH range = 29 to 37%).

Only four species were observed in total, and only one of these was observed during each survey (*Bufo speciosus* [Texas Toad]). Species richness on the three surveys was 3, 2, and 2, respectively. *Bufo speciosus* (Texas Toad) was always the most commonly observed species.

At CAVE, the monitoring transect was the Old Guano Trail, which was walked from the top of the trailhead near the cave amphitheater to approximately 3 km (1.9 mi) east and then back. This transect was run five mornings. Weather did not differ dramatically between transects (start temperature range = 22.6 to 25.0°C, RH range = 59 to 75%, cloud cover range = 0 to 5%; end temperature range = 27.9 to 34.4°C, RH range = 27 to 42%, cloud cover = 0 to 50%).

A total of seven species were observed, two of which were observed during every survey (*Aspidoscelis exsanguis* [Chihuahuan Spotted Whiptail] and *Sceloporus cowlesi* [Southwestern Fence Lizard]). Species richness during the five surveys was 6, 5, 3, 5, and 3, respectively. *Aspidoscelis exsanguis* (Chihuahuan Spotted Whiptail) was always one of the top two most common species found.

At FODA, we used the Tall Grass, North Ridge, and Hospital Canyon Trails as a transect loop. We ran this transect on five mornings. Temperatures remained fairly cool during the first and last surveys (start temperature range = 21.9 to 23.6°C, RH range = 50 to 61%, cloud cover range = 65 to 88%; end temperature range = 24.6 to 25.1°C, RH range = 40 to 57%, cloud cover range = 15 to 95%); the other three mornings were warmer (start temperature range = 24.0 to 26.9°C, RH range = 43 to 58%, cloud cover range = 15 to 75%; end temperature range = 28.6 to 30.1°C, RH range = 36 to 46%, cloud cover range = 5 to 20%).

A total of six species were observed, four of which were observed during every survey (*Aspidoscelis exsanguis* [Chihuahuan Spotted Whiptail], *Sceloporus cowlesi* [Southwestern Fence Lizard], *Sceloporus poinsettii poinsettii* [Northern Crevice Spiny Lizard], and *Urosaurus ornatus schmidti* [Big Bend Tree Lizard]. Species richness during the five surveys was 4, 5, 5, 5, and 3, respectively. *Urosaurus ornatus schmidti* (Big Bend Tree Lizard) was always the most common species found.

At GUMO, we used the McKittrick Canyon Trail as a transect. Starting at the trailhead, we surveyed to the Pratt Lodge on three mornings and from the trailhead to The Grotto on one morning. The first and third surveys were conducted on cool, overcast mornings (start temperature range = 18.1 to 21.0°C, RH range = 66 to 74%, cloud cover = 90%; end temperature range = 24.0 to 25.1°C, RH range = 42 to 58%, cloud cover range = 40 to 80%). The second and fourth surveys were conducted on warm, sunny mornings (start temperature range = 24.5 to 25.3°C, RH range = 51 to 54%, cloud cover = 0%; end temperature range = 28.4 to 31.7°C, RH range = 25 to 37%, cloud cover range = 3 to 5%).

Four species were observed, two of which were seen on every survey, *Aspidoscelis exsanguis* (Chihuahuan Spotted Whiptail) and *Sceloporus cowlesi* (Southwestern Fence Lizard). Species richness was 3 on every survey. *Aspidoscelis exsanguis* (Chihuahuan Spotted Whiptail) was always the most common species found.

These results indicate that apparent population parameters can change dramatically between surveys in a given year. Weather clearly has an important effect on the success of a given survey. Therefore, it is important to survey each area multiple times within a season. The data can then be pooled for the year to determine species composition, species richness, and relative abundance. Only a relatively small number of species (4 to 10) can be monitored in each area.

Ideally, if this method is used, permanent transects should be set up in several areas of each park and run every year. This will increase the number of species that can be monitored and also provide information about distribution.

Regardless of which methods are chosen for monitoring, we hope that the baseline data we have acquired regarding the current status of the herpetofauna of the National Parks of the Chihuahuan Desert will assist park managers to ensure that future generations will have the same opportunities we have had to enjoy the region's incredible and diverse array of wildlife.

Sources Cited

Brown, D.E. 1994. Biotic communities: Southwestern United States and Northwestern Mexico. University of Utah Press. Salt Lake City, Utah. 315 pp.

Conant, R. and J. T. Collins. 1998. A Field Guide to Reptiles and Amphibians, Eastern and Central North America. Houghton Mifflin Company, Boston.

Crother, B. I. (ed.). 2000. Scientific and Standard English Names of Amphibians and Reptiles of North America North of Mexico, with Comments Regarding Confidence in Our Understanding. SSAR Herpetological Circular 29.

Crother, B. I., J. Boundy, J. A. Campbell, K. DeQuieroz, D. Frost, D. M. Green, R. Highton, J. B. Iverson, R. W. McDiarmid, P. A. Meylan, T. W. Reeder, M. E. Seidel, J. W. Sites, Jr., S. G. Tilley, and D. B. Wake. 2003. Scientific and Standard English Names of Amphibians and Reptiles of North America North of Mexico: Update. Herpetological Review 34 (3): 196-203.

Dayton, G. 2002. Amphibians and Reptiles Checklist – Big Bend National Park. Big Bend Natural History Association, Big Bend National Park, TX.

Degenhardt, W. G., C. W. Painter, and A. H. Price. 1996. Amphibians and Reptiles of New Mexico. University of New Mexico Press, Albuquerque.

Grace, J. W. 1980. The Herpetofauna of Guadalupe Mountains National Park. Texas Tech University, Lubbock.

Leache, A. D. and T. W. Reeder. 2002. Molecular Systematics of the Eastern Fence Lizard (*Sceloporus undulatus*): A Comparison of Parsimony, Likelihood, and Bayesian Approaches. Systematic Biology 51(1): 44-68.

LoBello, R. L. 1976. Vertebrates of the Lake Amistad National Recreation Area. Master's thesis, presented to the Graduate Council, Sul Ross State University, Alpine, Texas.

Prival, D., J. Borgmeyer, and M. Wall. 2001. Herpetological Inventory of Sonoran Desert National Parks. Unpublished report. USGS Sonoran Desert Field Station, University of Arizona, Tucson.

Roemer, D. 2002. Draft Amphibians and Reptiles List for Carlsbad Caverns National Park, Eddy Co., New Mexico. Carlsbad Caverns National Park.

Stebbins, R. C. 2003. A Field Guide to Western Reptiles and Amphibians. Houghton Mifflin Company, Boston.

Stohlgren, T.J., and J.F. Quinn. 1992. An assessment of biotic inventories in western U.S. national parks. Natural Areas Journal 12:145-154.

Stohlgren, T.J., J.F. Quinn, M. Ruggiero, and G.S. Waggoner. 1995. Status of biotic inventories in U.S. national parks. Biological Conservation 71:97-106.

Werler, J. E. and J. R. Dixon. 2000. Texas Snakes. University of Texas Press, Austin.

NPS 960/110293, September 2011